Whatever She Wants

Whatever She Wants

True Confessions of a Male Escort

ANDREW ROSETTA

EBURY
PRESS

1 3 5 7 9 10 8 6 4 2

Published in 2009 by Ebury Press, an imprint of Ebury Publishing
A Random House Group Company

The Random House Group Limited Reg. No. 954009

Addresses for companies within the Random House Group can be
found at www.randomhouse.co.uk

A CIP catalogue record for this book is available from the
British Library

Penguin Random House is committed to a sustainable future for
our business, our readers and our planet. This book is made from
Forest Stewardship Council® certified paper.

Printed and bound in Great Britain by Clays Ltd, Elcograf S.p.A.

ISBN 9780091928148

To buy books by your favourite authors and register for offers visit
www.rbooks.co.uk

Contents

To Dr Laura Agustín,
whose book *Sex at the Margins* inspired
me to write my own

This is a true account of my life and the people and situations I have known and lived through. Where appropriate, names, personal details, geography and chronology have been altered to help preserve the anonymity of those involved. In particular, 'Innocence' is an amalgamation of several women I have encountered in the sex industry. This is to enable the voices and stories of the people involved to come through without blowing their cover. My intention throughout is never to embarrass or expose anyone but to faithfully portray my life as an escort.

Bad Workmen Always Blame Their Tools

I've been told I have a beautiful penis. That's what's been said, and while I think I can tell the difference between an ugly penis and a beautiful one, I don't know about my own. Someone also once said it had the biggest girth they'd ever seen, though I know that's not true. But size is important, and, yes, I'm lucky not to have to worry about that.

My penis is uncircumcized, which is either a bonus or a drawback depending on who you are with. An Iranian girl once played with it for hours, as if it were a toy, but then she'd never seen an uncircumcised penis before. It's seven inches long, or so I tell my clients when they ask. But then all escorts add an inch when they talk about size, just as they always subtract five years from their age, which makes me twenty-nine. Luckily I look young enough and my penis is big enough to pull off the exaggeration. It's supposed to be a plus, a big penis with a wide girth, but it depends on who you are with. Certainly, convention dictates that it is a good thing. But then convention also says it's what you do with it that matters, not how big it is. In fact, I've discovered that women *do* care about size. But I'd never describe myself as some sort of sex god, or as having this amazing penis and knowing exactly what to do with it.

I am a male escort. I've been voted the best escort in Britain, and I have a statue of a golden cock with wings and a certificate to remind me of this. I have needed reminding. I've loved being an escort, or at least loved the life it's given me: not just the trappings, but the actual day-to-day life. But it's not all been good. I've been blackmailed, threatened and suffered severe depression and panic attacks. I may yet be in jail as you read this book.

On the other hand, I was also in debt ten years ago and now I have assets that run in excess of a million pounds. Business, over the years, has been mostly very, very good. To give you one example, though I admit it is an extreme one, I once did twenty jobs over two days. That was back in 2001, right in the middle of the peak years, and I calculated that I came sixteen times in twenty-four hours. You can try not to come during a job, but often the client wants to see 'it', and whatever else, it closes the deal. They come – you come; it's done. But after a lot of orgasms over a short period of time it becomes mechanical. Hardly anything comes out. I'm sure it can't be good for you. Certainly, too forced an orgasm is not a particularly enjoyable one. But just when you think you can't ever come again, you keep going and you find you can.

It's like long-distance running. You hit the wall but if you force yourself to keep going you get past it. But it takes a big effort and sometimes I feel pushed too far. One client, called Cheryl, used to want me to come two or three times in a single session. I like Cheryl and she's been a good, regular client, but there is demanding and then there is: back off, I'm dying here. But you can't tell clients that. You can't say: I'm knackered and bored and sore and the worry and hard work of maintaining an erection all the time is not nothing, you know. This is less of a problem for female escorts, or rather they have different problems.

It's a little-known fact that female escorts are paid twice, sometimes three times more than their male counterparts. I accept this as my lot because the market sets the price. This friend of mine, a clinical psychologist, told me she gets paid less than her exact equivalent male colleagues, which is clearly unfair. But the situation in escorting is the reverse. In the oldest profession in the world, men earn less per hour than their female counterparts, and the difference between day rates is even greater.

Sometimes clients want to see a male and a female escort at the same time – this is called doing a 'duo' – either because they want to join in on a threesome or simply because they like to watch. Sometimes they want a male escort and lots of females. That's when it becomes more of a 'party'. Usually an agent organizes the party, but not always, and if I'm the one who has called the female escorts and brought them in on a job, then the girlz (escorts use the terms 'girlz' and 'boyz' but of course always referring to men and women over the age of eighteen) might say, as we are triumphantly sharing out the spoils in a taxi on the way home: let's go fifty-fifty on this one. But not always. With one of my more extravagant clients, Mile High Bob, the girls get double my fee, even though I'm always the one organizing everything. Though when I say organize, it isn't exactly forward planned. No to-do list is ever drawn up. Mostly, with escorting, a client calls up and wants to see you *right now*.

I mentioned Cheryl. Mostly I have regular slots with Cheryl – I'm slotted in her diary between her standing weekly appointments at the hairdresser, nail salon and tanning centre. But sometimes once a week isn't enough for Cheryl. Sometimes she calls me up and wants to see me immediately, never mind what I'm in the middle of, or who else I've promised to see, and because she's one of my best clients I always do my best to accommodate her 'needs'. Cheryl found me through one of my early London lonely heart ads, and she has stuck with me through thick and thin. Of course, you're not strictly allowed to advertise as an escort in these magazine sections, but many turn a blind eye if you are discreet and never any trouble. My ad ran, like many of them do, along the lines of: 'sexy and smart financially challenged fit guy requests mature lady with resources to aid him in his need'. These are all but coming to an end in magazines but have their Internet equivalent on sites like Gumtree and Craigslist. Needless to say, it is imperative when you receive follow-up phone calls that you make your position absolutely clear and not mislead anyone. There is enough trouble around in this business without issuing it with an invitation, and, besides, misrepresenting yourself is both illegal and bad for business in the long run.

I didn't have to explain much to Cheryl. She understood perfectly what I was advertising. She liked the idea of paying someone for sex, and continued to like it for many years, much to my benefit. But I don't drop everything for Cheryl just because she's such a good and loyal customer. There's more to it than that. Simply put, sex with Cheryl is like fireworks.

She's a larger-than-life Essex girl, our Cheryl, in her late forties when I first met her, blonde and blousy, tanned and tarty, and because she is married to a successful, if slightly shady figure who runs casinos, not short of a few bob.

Her husband, an old school East-ender made good –

honestly, the epitome of what Guy Ritchie's characters are based on – not only knows about our sessions, but pays for them. He doesn't want to sleep with Cheryl anyway. He's got his own mistress – 'the slut', according to Cheryl – whom he's been seeing for years and with whom he even has a child. None with Cheryl though (for reasons I assume are physical). But if Cheryl is denied a lot emotionally, she compensates for it by spending up a storm. What else is she going to do with her day? She's never worked and doesn't have kids so she keeps busy looking after *every* bit of herself.

Nor is 'body work' her only expense. She drives a classic sixties sports car, wears expensive clothes and always, apparently, has the latest handbag on her arm, whatever that is. Her Essex house, with its thick-pile carpets and white leather sofa suites, is one of many, she tells me proudly on my first out-call, and though many of Cheryl's stories seem incredible, over the years they have all proved to be true as far as I can ascertain, which tallies, since she's the sort of person who wears her heart on her sleeve and calls a spade a spade. The stories involve real wealth, real crime, real prison, real violence and real estate. Her husband, whom I've spoken to on the phone, is clearly not a man to be disrespected. What is also clear is that Cheryl loves sex, and loves having sex with me. In her head I'm her posh Cambridge-educated boy toy, my world as much of a mystery to her as hers, with its own particular codes and lore and rules and status symbols, is to me.

I don't find Cheryl's inch-high white carpets, tiger-print lingerie and Barbie-pink boudoir-like bedroom a turn-on, but *she does* and that's what matters. And her being so highly sexed is exciting if occasionally mildly frightening. She's medium height, slim and womanly shaped, with huge breasts and large nipples that are very sensitive to being licked and sucked. Nor am I the only one doing the sucking. Cheryl's lips are as voluptuous as her shape. If my body is the road map to peace, she takes the scenic path unhurried and with abandon, tracing her route with her tongue. She has this trick, in the course of giving a blow job, where at some point she gently and firmly licks round the rim of my cock, sucks the head quite hard and then finally takes the whole stem in her throat. Trust me, this works. So much so that sometimes I have to remind myself that I am the one working for a living. So, sometimes, does she, crazy as it is, and though we have nothing but sex in common I have found myself strangely fancying her from time to time over the years. There have been times when I've had to discipline myself not to allow her to run over time or not pay properly.

I think part of Cheryl wishes that she and I could run off into the sunset with her husband's millions. In some senses that would have been fine for me. Once I started to take escorting seriously I was open to the idea of finding a wealthy sugar mummy to take care of me financially. But not one with a husband, or at least not a husband who has access to a couple of serious heavies when he wants. Even if he did approve of my services. And anyway I don't think Cheryl ever thought about it with real longing. Mostly she was after me for one thing and one thing only. She wasn't bothered by my psychological or physiological needs, and nor did she have to be.

Unlike many people you encounter in escorting, Cheryl was not out to save me. She's more concerned with her own sexual needs, about which she is absolutely straight-talking and whose satisfaction she is more than happy to pay for. 'You're five minutes late,' she'd say as she picked me up from the Cambridge train. 'And I've had to sit in my own little wet patch waiting for you. I'm gagging for it,' she'd add, with an infectious, filthy, joyous laugh, starting up her gas-guzzler with one hand and putting the other firmly on my crotch, a bundle of notes adding an extra layer of excitement between her hand and my groin.

Whenever we get to her house, Cheryl is ready to go. Small talk doesn't interest her and she doesn't need a glass of wine to loosen up. It's like she's on heat. She doesn't even want to be kissed, unlike most female clients, who are often interested in being touched and held and stroked and 'loved' as much as actually fucked. Not Cheryl. 'Darling, you've got your money,' she says with a chortle. 'Now let's see what you can do with that lovely cock.' I feel suitably objectified as she drags me upstairs, her shirt already off, her saucy bra straining to hold its load, her nipples taut with desire. As soon as we get to the bed – satin sheets of course – she pulls down my trousers and sticks my cock so far down her throat I wonder if I'm going to push out the other side. But, God, does she know how to give a blow job!

Mostly in escorting what I do is no great shakes. Some finger fiddling here, a tongue insertion there. Nothing that is going to cause the earth to move. But sex with Cheryl is like something you see in a porn movie. Her pussy is perfectly shaved. She really is as wet as her talk. She throws me onto the bed and mounts me with unbridled enthusiasm, all the while telling me how much she wants me inside her. She really can come and come. Her body shakes, she screams out, her pussy spasms over and over again, releasing so much female ejaculate that both my body and the bed sheets are soaked with it!

I used to think female ejaculation was an urban myth (invented, I thought, in the minds of men) so the first time I had sex with Cheryl I assumed she'd wet herself when she climaxed. How wrong I was. Likewise, I didn't have much experience with multiple orgasm (multiple being more than one in my and most men's minds) but Cheryl builds up from orgasm to orgasm until after about forty minutes or so she can be in such a state of heightened excitement that she hardly needs to be touched to come. Simply stroking her inner thigh again can set her off in an additional explosion. I'm not exaggerating. The trick to get her there is to *stay hard and not come*, which is not as easy as it might sound, even for a professional escort. To fuck continuously for two hours while your partner goes through forty-odd orgasms can be a serious challenge, especially when you don't know how you might feel on a Thursday at 11 a.m. You might be tired, hungover, recovering from having been up all night with your own partner or another client, have the flu or feel stressed out. But come rain or shine, Cheryl expects her superman to perform.

Still, I'm not the miracle worker she thinks I am. My cock has its work cut out with Cheryl but what turns her on to such an extent is what is going on in *her head*. I answer her fantasies. I'm under her control. She treats me as a sex object quite openly. I don't necessarily like that but it's what I've signed up for and I know it's part of what gets her going. She's hired me for hot, dirty sex and so that's what her head tells her body it's getting, and that in turn is what then happens.

Cheryl is an important client for me. She makes me feel sexy and good at my job, and that's important in escorting because you have to deal with a lot of anonymity, subterfuge and stories – both yours and your clients' – and secrets produce stress. That's OK, and if you want a cosy time at work with regular chats around the water cooler about the latest reality TV show, escorting isn't for you. But it was, more and more, I discovered, for me. Still, if you'd told me this twelve years ago when I was a virgin training to become a born-again Christian church leader and about to start a degree in religious history at a good university, I'd have claimed you were insane.

CHAPTER 2

Sex God = Sex + God

I'm a nice, middle-class boy with a master's degree. I come from a stable and loving family and a close-knit community. My family aren't just upright and moral, they are born-again evangelical Christians; I myself trained to become a church leader. I was a virgin until I was twenty-three. So why on earth did I decide to become an escort? And if the short answer is: as a way to get money fast, then the next question must be: how come I am still doing it, and as a full-time job moreover, ten years later? Winning ruddy prizes for it in fact. And getting into severe trouble at various times over the years. But here's the thing – if you decide to make your living as an escort you take an oath, and it runs along the lines of: '*So be it.*' I made my oath in 1998, two years after my first escort job. Mine went: '*So be it to whatever end.*'

The problem isn't that what I do is illegal. It isn't.

Soliciting is illegal and so is working out of a house with a friend – a brothel, in other words – but being paid for your time and paying or being paid for sex is entirely legal in the UK (although this could change in 2009). However, the entire industry is unregulated and, worse, unnecessarily criminalized at the edges. You have to know that, when you become an escort, and for many, including me for a while, that's part of the appeal. That's why you take the oath. It's a bargain. You get the life, but it comes at a price.

I didn't know any of this when I placed my first ad in my local newspaper in 1996 when I was twenty-three years old. But then I didn't know a lot of things back then. In fact, I felt entirely lost. That was a new feeling for me. Unlike many, I didn't have a confusing adolescence. It wasn't always easy, but it wasn't confusing. I was on a firm path heading in a straight line towards a certain future.

I was born and grew up in a small picture-postcard Area of Outstanding Natural Beauty in Cornwall, with my older brother and loving parents. My father worked as a chartered accountant and my mother was a linguist and a department head in a primary school. Both go to a modern church. Bible study was a regular but not oppressive part of our childhood.

Home life was stable and secure and my brother and I knew we were loved, but my schooldays weren't always happy. I am dyslexic, and though I've learnt to cope with it now, I found it hard when I was young. At primary school I was put into a class with kids with behavioural problems; as a result I fell in with the tearaways. And if I was going to be labelled bad, I inevitably began to reason, then I might as well live up to it. Anyway, I preferred being cast as naughty rather than thick, and I quickly discovered that if I told people I was dyslexic then their knee-jerk reaction was to limit me. So I learnt ways of concealing my dyslexia. It was an early lesson in something I would come to excel at: how to succeed when the system is weighted against you, how to find an alternative route to success. If you can't beat it, join it, as the saying goes, and if you can't join it, work it.

One of the ways I succeeded in primary school was by being good at sport. It was my rugby teacher who first said to me: 'You're not thick, Andrew, you just can't write well and your reading is slow, but you're not thick.' His words helped me. I put a lot of time and effort into excelling at sports, but while I knew that using my body in a physically challenging way was something I was passionate about, it was not my calling. I found that when I was fifteen.

I was fifteen when I had the experience of being born again. For nine years I was a seriously, wildly committed Christian. Embarrassingly so, when I look back. as I believed it all. That was the life I was going to lead, and so not only did I go to church but eventually I began working for the church and trained to become a church leader.

Being a church leader in the evangelical churches is like being a Baptist or Methodist minister. You serve the same function as a vicar in many ways. Becoming a church leader was Plan A for me. There was no Plan B. I did a leadership course in North London, studied Religion at Anglia Ruskin University in Cambridge, and when I had finished my degree moved to a large town in the northeast with the mission to start and eventually lead two new congregations there.

So you can imagine how I felt when it all went wrong. I was given access to what went on behind the scenes of the Church and what I saw – church leaders lying, power play and corruption – disillusioned me. I couldn't believe it when I first heard a church leader slagging off – and lying about – someone he was supposed to be supporting. And this sort of thing fed into and confirmed deep doubts I was having about the very foundations of the Christian faith. The initial euphoria of having been born again had long since worn off and I was meeting a lot of new people who were introducing me to different ways of seeing the world than what I grew up with. Some of these new ideas rocked the very core of my belief. There are a thousand reasons for how you get to the point of saying: I don't believe this is true; but after nine years and a lot of angst I decided it just wasn't working. It wasn't that it was good for nothing, it just wasn't as good as it purported to be and the church no better than any other group of good people.

By 1996 I was leading my life feeling enormous tension as doubts about Christianity and the place of God in life and belief came up against the real world. And if being born again was the most transformative period of my life, the growing feeling that we are alone in the universe, that there is no Creator, no divine being to give life meaning, was taking shape. Without God there were no absolutes, and if there were no absolutes, I reasoned, then what was right and what was wrong? And I had drawn an awful lot of direction from faith in God, but without Him, where did that leave me?

Added to that is the fact that it's a struggle to lead a Christian life and avoid temptation. By this time I had been seeing a girl called Rebecca for three years. Though we fancied each other like mad and both fancied sex like crazy, left to our own devices, we didn't do it. We had played around and 'petted' but we abstained from actual sex because we weren't married and the faith we had was stronger even than our desires.

That's usually why people leave the Church: their desires get the better of them, which is pretty human really. They just gradually start to do stuff they feel they shouldn't, and slowly phase out of the Church or get too busy and other things become a priority. For me, there were a thousand questions going unanswered, the church leaders' behaviour not the least, and I had learnt through their behaviour that being a Christian didn't necessarily mean you behaved like one, and perhaps there were other ways to live one's life. It took a long time for me to come to the decision to leave the Church. But I was the blue-eyed boy of my Church's future and I wasn't going to fade away.

I asked my church leader and my greatest role model if I could meet him and his wife privately. I had something important I wanted to discuss with them, I said. Only when they arrived I didn't say anything. Instead I put on the Irving Berlin song 'There May Be Trouble Ahead'. 'Let's have a little dance,' I said as Nat King Cole sang out the famous lyrics. 'There's going to be some trouble ahead,' I said as we danced. 'I'm leaving. Leaving the job. I'm not just leaving the church, but the whole thing. Everything.

Basically I danced out of the Church and my life as I had known it to that day, and it felt great. If being born again was the best feeling I have ever experienced, and losing my faith was the worst, then liberating myself from this disappointment came close to the euphoria of discovering God in the first place. All at once I felt this sense of freedom. My feeling was: I can rule the world, I can be an art thief, I can sleep with whomever I like, I can travel the world, rob a bank, buy a house, buy a street of houses, I can do whatever I want to do, nothing is impossible for me. I had that youthful feeling of immortality.

I have done a couple of those things too, but not all at once and not immediately after leaving the Church. I was euphoric, yes, but there was also reality and reality catches up with euphoria fairly quickly in my experience. My reality was that I had student loans to pay off, no money, no direction, no plans and no connections. My family, at first puzzled and disbelieving of my decision to leave the Christian faith, soon came to accept what I had done, but I still felt alone and at sea. I was reading Mario Puzo's *The Godfather* at the time, and the book was hugely influential on my thinking because it showed me there was another way around any kind of system. I'm not saying I immediately decided to go and join a criminal network. No. It just made me think that there were other ways of doing things. I was ready for anything, willing to do whatever it took to get where I wanted, and I realized that maybe I was going to have to take an unconventional path to get there.

The only problem was, what path? What *would* it take? And so I flailed around for a time. But if I felt lost I also knew, somewhere inside me, that I would find my way, and so I prepared myself. I became incredibly fit. I ran, went to the gym and swam long distances every day. I signed on to the dole and in between collecting my giro I cycled all over the country. I hitchhiked with my bicycle to Ireland and cycled there, then spent four months cycling through Spain from south to north with almost no money in my pocket. My determination and my will as well as my muscles and my stamina grew stronger and stronger.

The thing about me is that I'm a natural non-conformist. Does that sound like an odd thing to say, given that I was a serious, committed Christian for nine years? While it's true that you might be accepted within your Church, being the sort of born-again Christian I was goes against the values of your peers and society. People think it's OK to poke fun at Christians in the way they wouldn't do of practitioners of other religions, so for me there was always that sense of standing just outside the borders of normal society. Cycling through Spain, travelling long distances on hot, dusty roads, gave me a lot of time to think about the direction my life was heading…

When I returned to England I placed an escort ad in the local paper. Why? Looking back, at the time I didn't really have direction. Because I knew I had to do something and I didn't know what else to do. A degree in Religion doesn't exactly open doors to a vocation, especially if you've just closed the door to the Church yourself. I'd done holiday jobs and unpaid 'work experience' but that didn't amount to much and anyway I'd never really felt comfortable doing that sort of work. Having once known exactly what I wanted to do, having had a vocation and felt how fulfilling that could be, working in a nine-to-five job just to pay the bills felt like slipping into mediocrity to me.

With the loss of my religion came the prospect of new opportunities, opportunities that weren't necessarily the ones that my parents would pick out for me.

I went to the university's postgraduate unit and did their half-day psychometric careers tests. Two careers were suggested to me far and away above anything else: to become either a Baptist minister or an officer in the Marines. Well, I'd tried one and didn't fancy being shouted at in the other. One thing I did know was that people fancied me, and although I'd never really given in to it in the Christian years, I knew this could influence people. I decided to use it.

I ran an ad in the local paper, near where I lived with my parents (yes, after I finished my degree and left the church I moved back home). It really wasn't a big deal. I didn't debate it or struggle with what I was doing, nor did I think it mattered that I was still, technically, a virgin. I just went ahead and did it. 'Male Escort -- out-calls only – Robert', the ad ran, with my mobile number printed in bold type. Not long after it appeared several men called asking for Robert, which meant that I had to explain that Robert wasn't gay and didn't take male clients. It was disheartening. Where were the women encouraged by magazines like *Cosmopolitan* to explore their fantasies with a young stud like me? Why weren't they calling?

And then my first did. A woman who wanted me to have sex with her while her husband watched. He was just going to sit in the corner of the room, she said. He certainly wasn't interested in any gay stuff, she confirmed, so it was all for the better that I wasn't either. How much did I charge? That was a good question. I had no idea either of how much I was worth or what someone would be willing to pay to have me fuck them while their husband looked on. I'd never met or spoken to anyone in the sex industry apart from those who had converted to Christianity (and they were pretty thin on the ground), and though I'd seen ads in the back of the paper before (hence my having the idea to place my own), none of them quoted a price. 'Would thirty-five pounds be acceptable?' I asked. It was a rather random figure but while it didn't seem too outlandish it was more than I could earn pulling pints for a night's work. It would, she said.

That's how I found myself sitting in my parents' car, which I had borrowed 'to go and meet a friend from university', outside a magnolia-coloured house in a new flat-pack estate, thinking about what I was about to do and who I was going to meet. What happened if the couple were mad psycho killers? The thought had occurred to me before I'd left and so I'd written a note for my brother and sealed it in a brown envelope with instructions that it should only be opened if I had not returned by 1 a.m. My brother worked in a student bar in the beautiful, quaint middle-class town where we were brought up and wouldn't be back till after midnight, which left me plenty of time to do the job and get home, if it was indeed my destiny to remain in one piece.

When I arrived at their address my heart was racing. I felt watched, not just in a paranoid way – though that too – but because everywhere I drove I, along with the rest of the country, was being stared at by New Labour's red 'demon eyes', as portrayed by the Conservative Party. The Conservatives were running a negative campaign with posters saying 'New Labour New Danger' in the months before the 1997 May General Election. 'New labour new danger' struck me as a potently appropriate slogan to accompany me on my first foray into escorting.

I looked at my clients' house. The window frames were white plastic. The house was semi-detached, pebble-dashed and identical to all its neighbours. It was the embodiment of conformity, an ordinary house in suburbia. Who were these people calling out a male escort for a spot of Saturday night entertainment? I felt curious and excited and nervous.

I rang the doorbell. A woman answered. She was some-what older than me – I suppose some part of me was hoping for Jennifer Aniston. When you're twenty-three, thirty-eight (as I found out she was) seems much older, but she looked quite sexy in a sweet kind of way. She seemed embarrassed for a moment, but then she smiled warmly and I thought: OK, this is OK. She led me into her front room and her husband shuffled in wearing new cheap jeans. We exchanged pleasantries while I looked around. A bottle of cheap red wine sat on a seventies coffee table with the veneer starting to bubble, and scattered everywhere were photographs of teenage children, grandparents and happy family outings. I sat opposite them, accepted a glass of wine and switched on the charm. I thought: this I can do.

We talked a little about their town, the weather, local shopping and what they did for a living. They were police officers, they said. I kept a straight face but inwardly I nearly spat out my wine. *Police?* I felt a sinking thud in my stomach. I couldn't have heard that right. Police?

Police officers, the woman repeated, making a guilty-as-charged-but-who-cares-let-the-party-begin face. She pointed to the photographs behind me showing the happy couple in younger days dressed head to toe in navy blue and beaming with pride at their 'passing out' – a police graduation ceremony to you and me. I felt faint. Then, just to really turn me on, they both showed me their warrant cards. Note to any police officers thinking of hiring fresh-faced new escorts: don't tell them you're in the police! They tend to get nervous!

I was utterly deflated. And even more nervous because now I was also wondering if this was an undercover bust on me, the rampaging prostitute of the south-west. Nerves make me soft. I had been doing so well, I'd even been feeling a little horny. Now all I could think was: this isn't going to work. I could feel my cock, all eager and semi-hard moments before, crawl back down. And the softer I felt, the more nervous I got. I thought of the note I had left for my brother. I imagined the clock striking one while I was at the police station and my brother was opening the envelope and divulging its contents to my mother.

My mother! That was a convenient thought – just in case there was any danger of my cock ever getting hard again. 'Right, lad,' Cheap Jeans said. 'Can I have a word?' I imagined the cuffs tightening on my wrists. 'OK,' he went on, 'in a minute I'll go up stairs, go into our en-suite bathroom and close the door. Michelle will then bring you upstairs. If you want to kiss her down here, I don't mind, but don't take too long about it, save it for the bedroom. When I hear you on the bed I'll give you a couple of minutes and then I'll come in and sit in the corner.' It was like a sergeant giving orders to a new recruit or an arresting officer on a Saturday night in the cells.

Apparently it didn't seem as if I was about to be busted, but all I really wanted to do was get the hell out of there. Michelle was looking at me as Cheap Jeans gave me my instructions. She suggested I take my jacket off and smiled as I did so. Then she suggested I remove my T-shirt before I follow her up in five minutes. I removed my top and downed a second glass of wine. 'I'm really looking forward to you fucking me hard and long,' she said in a stage whisper as she turned to leave.

OK. Less boring. Still nothing doing though. I said she looked beautiful and, as she gave me an erotic look I found hammy, I managed to force out a smile. I knew it wasn't convincing.

In contrast to her husband she was less nimble on her feet as she plodded upstairs. I could imagine her on the beat. I looked at their uniformed photographs on the mantelpiece and considered doing a runner. But that's not my style. Fuck it, I thought, how hard can it be? Come on! Come on, cock! I fumbled for a suitable fantasy, anything to help me get it up. It's funny how sometimes you have to really force your sexual imagination to work. Here I was about to fuck a stranger, watched by her copper partner – a sure-fire winning fantasy for many – and yet I was struggling to even think about sex. Never mind that it was going to be my first time.

The clock ticked, light and plastically. I forced myself to concentrate. I felt ridiculous sitting on the sofa now in my pants, stroking myself, and still wondering if this wasn't some judicial sting. I worked through a few of my fantasies and there, at last, a stirring. It was modest at first, but at least it proved my cock was still alive. I touched my nipples. I've always had ridiculously sensitive nipples if touched gently. I thanked God that they weren't failing me.

There was no time to lose. I jumped up and headed for the stairs, taking them two at a time. I arrived at the doorway to the bedroom like an athletic rugby player in my white pants that concealed my not-so-confident stiffy. Michelle was lying on the bed in a dimly lit white Formica bedroom with mirrored built-in wardrobes. It could have been my parents' room. It was so ordinary, so domestic, so normal. But there was nothing normal about the smell in the room. It was like being confronted by a firewall of pheromone heat. The room was thick with the fug of it. 'I want it all and I want it now and we're not going to stop fucking till tomorrow,' she said as she lay waiting for me on the bed.

I felt out of my body from the moment we kissed, but not in a dizzy, passionate way. Her tongue, her breasts, her hairless pussy turned me off. My mouth felt like it was full of cotton wool or I'd just had a filling at the dentist. I opened my eyes mid-kiss. What the fuck am I doing here? I haven't got a hard-on. I cannot get a hard-on. I started to panic as the thought that my first night as an escort didn't bode well for the rest of my career ran through my mind – this, of course, didn't help me maintain my erection. Now I had two things to hide – the fact that I couldn't get it up and the fact that I was horribly embarrassed that I couldn't do this most primal of things. Oh God! Can you pray to God to ask you to be a better prostitute? I wondered.

I tried a trick, the principles of which I learnt in primary school playing rugby. 'Covering' is what you do if you need to slow down a rugby game so your team can regroup for a moment and try to regain their confidence. You stall the action a bit, mess about and slow things down when you sense your team have lost control. In these circumstances panic can quickly set in, and within a moment a strong team can be overrun. But if one person or a small group take the initiative they can 'cover' the game by playing for a bit of time while the rest of the team catches breath, comes back on side and realizes things aren't so bad. The trick is to remain in possession of the ball while stalling the other team. This was my plan: cover, play for time, stall, regain confidence, calm down and try again. It didn't work. I couldn't get an erection. Not a sausage. It was excruciatingly embarrassing.

It must have been terrible for her. She had clearly made an effort for me and my reaction was to go limp at the sight of her. We tried a little longer. Each time she told me to relax, I could feel her confidence wane. My confidence was shattered too, and I wasn't performing like I should. I should have been leading her, kissing her neck gently, stroking her breasts, teasing her clit with my tongue. Christ, if I couldn't fuck her like a porn star the least I might have done was to make her feel beautiful, but it seemed I couldn't even manage that. So now, added to my embarrassment and humiliation was guilt at not being able to make this perfectly nice and sexy woman feel good.

Inevitably, when her husband came into the bedroom

'to watch', things went from bad to worse. He'd paid me to give his wife a good seeing to and my whole body was rejecting her. He told me to stop. The bedside light went on. I sat on the edge of the bed for a moment turning red. Not just my face but my entire body. Red. Cheap Jeans told me to go downstairs. I think I said 'I'm sorry' as I left the room. Naked. I returned to the living room, sat on the sofa and wondered how to extricate myself from this situation.

When Cheap Jeans eventually appeared he told me his wife was lying on the bed inconsolable, that I had destroyed her self-esteem and that she now 'felt like a dog'. He told me that I was entirely unprofessional (he was right), but he spoke as if he was giving me a caution, which, to be honest, gave the situation a sort of ridiculous absurdity. Between that and the dog comment I had to stop myself from smirking. He certainly wasn't smiling.

I mumbled something about it being my first time, but he was having none of it. And it wasn't as if he could get the satisfaction of asking for his money back – I was so green that I hadn't learnt the first rule of escorting: get the money up front. If I could have given him his money back, I would. Cheap Jeans told me he wanted me out of his house. Believe me I couldn't wait to leave either, but to my own surprise I stood there defiantly. He looked at me, his eyes filled with wrath.

'What?' he said, even though I hadn't said anything.

'I've left my pants upstairs,' I said. Actually I wasn't entirely sure where most of my clothes were. Why hadn't I thought ahead? I should have placed my clothes in a neat pile by the door of the downstairs room, so that if necessary I could have thrown them on quickly and made a swift exit. I wondered if he was going to kick me out naked. Explaining that to my mum and dad as I handed back the car keys would not be a laugh.

Cheap Jeans looked at me for a moment. 'Right,' he finally said wearily before disappearing upstairs. I could hear their muffled voices. She was clearly very upset. Eventually he came back down with my pants, holding them delicately between two fingers as if they might contaminate him. Putting them on was like stepping into something sodden and cold and horrible. He didn't take his eyes off me.

'I'm not sure where my trousers are.'

'You idiot boy.' I thought he was going to hit me. Certainly, he spat out the word 'boy'. But instead he told me to stay where I was while he trundled off to find my clothes. After what seemed like an age he returned and threw them at me. He told me to dress as quickly as I could, and when I was done he held the front door open. I heard it slam behind me.

And that was that. My first job as an escort and I felt stupid and embarrassed and as broke as when I started, only minus the petrol money.

Once I got home, I managed to retrieve the brown envelope with the note to my brother before he saw it. Small mercies, I suppose. I resolved to remove my advert and never repeat such ridiculousness.

Tonight We Will Fake Love

In early 1997, the whole of Britain seemed to be gearing up towards a huge sea change. I was glad when New Labour won the May General Election with such a landslide victory. There was an energy in the air, anything seemed possible, and the whole country appeared to be going off together in a new direction. My own life seemed to be too.

I was still a bit lost though. Added to which, the door into an escorting career – you know, the one *everyone* gets tempted to go through every so often – now seemed utterly shut. So I did what anyone leaving university with a fairly useless degree and no idea about what do to next does: teach English as a foreign language. Only it's less of a standard thing to do if, like me, you are rather dyslexic. Getting a Business English certificate plus a grade-3 MBQ and TEFL certificate in four weeks and then teaching for eighteen months in the top schools in both Spain and Oxford was the most difficult thing I have ever done. I would have been failed or fired on the spot if discovered, and a dyslexic is easy to spot if you're a linguist! Therefore, I kept my dyslexia under wraps and I was doubly conscientious in preparing my classes focusing on pronunciation and business classes rather than spelling and grammar. It was with some pleasure and not a little irony that I discovered that my classes' performance was above average in the schools ratings in their finals, even pipping some of the senior teachers to the post in what was a very competitive academic establishment.

The reason I'm telling you all this is to give you insight into how someone can learn to cope in a business like escorting where so much bluff, street wisdom, self-confidence and talent is needed not only to do the physical job but also to cope mentally and emotionally, dealing either with keeping it a secret or with facing social judgment and exclusion. Being excluded from normal classes and put in a 'remedial' class when you are better than averagely intelligent, and struggling and succeeding eventually in academically focused schools is actually a very good training ground; so is being labelled 'different'. Sociologists have a theory, which is if you label people enough they will start acting out the label. I owe a huge debt to the many English teachers who have had to suffer me over the years!

There were other good things happening too: in 1997, early in the New Year, I lost my virginity with Rebecca, the girlfriend I had had for three years in my late teens. She came to visit one evening while I was studying for my TEFL qualification in Oxford. We'd stayed friends and both left the Church at around the same time. When Rebecca came to stay, we both decided we deserved to temporarily rekindle the sexual part of our romance and do what we should have done years before. It was wonderful. For first-time sex to have been with someone who mattered so much to me was, in retrospect, a real gift. Sex like many things can so easily be overused, misused or abused, but however fumbling and rubbish we were (me more than her) it all felt right and great, all the more for having waited for so many years; we respected each other, and we were both discovering sex together. Afterwards we lay in bed together, giggling how it was so very unplanned but it felt so right. My virginity had, by this time, become something of a burden – I was ten years behind many of my best friends. Abstinence doesn't necessarily mean deprivation: there are a lot of pluses to waiting, not least that it confers an incredible sense of mystery on the act. And when I finally got to that point, the sex itself was amazing – at least it was for me.

If I had been keen on the idea of sex before, I was now positively wild about it. To my joy – and it was about the only thing I was taking joy in – it seemed that I wasn't a failure at attracting the opposite sex. What do I look like? Well, if you're a customer ringing me up for the first time I'll be brief and succinct. I'm just under six foot with a muscular, athletic build, smooth tanned skin, deep blue eyes and blond hair. I'm seven inches down below, uncut and I cost more than many can afford for an hour's pleasure. Only of course I didn't have customers at this time; nor, after the fiasco with the police officers. did I think I ever would. I was simply revelling in the sort of easy, free, unattached, by now unwatched-by-God sex that lots of people have in their early twenties.

Unattached sex, yes, but not unimportant. I don't believe in casual sex. What's casual about such a wonderful, fantastic thing, even if you're having it with someone you barely know and don't love? You are still driven by desire. It's still an astonishingly intimate act. You can't buy that, by the way. Sure, in time, I learn to rent out something that looks a bit like it. But actually making love with a client? Forget it.

Even if you don't love someone you've slept with freely and simply because you share chemistry and both want to, you've still formed a bond. You have to honour that. Let me tell you a story to show you what I mean. The pupils I taught in the English school in Oxford were visiting Italian kids and had accompanying Italian staff. One of them was a gorgeous teacher called Margarita. I fancied her immediately and we managed a bit of a two-night stand, which helped alleviate the tedium of the school's twenty-four-hour routine (teachers and students: we all boarded at the school). Somehow, the very old-fashioned head teacher, on the Italian side, found out that Margarita had committed the heinous crime of having a romance with one of the English staff and decided she needed to put a stop to it. Not that it was any of her business. It's not like we did it in on-duty hours or invited our pupils to watch us go at it.

So why did Margarita come to my room in tears one day? She told me that her boss had slagged her off in the staff room in front of half the Italian staff who were there having coffee, and had taken her off the teaching rota and given her a load of specially devised teacher-in-doghouse chores instead. The fling, which she denied, had also been leaked to the Italian kids and you can imagine how fast that would travel. *I was furious.* At lunch the next day, when the whole school – staff and pupils – were in the dining hall, I collected two glasses of full-fat milk from the milk station and made sure they were full to the brim. I found a reason to go past the Italian teachers' top table (Italian and English teachers ate separately from the pupils and from each other in old-style long tables perpendicular to the main rows), where I 'slipped' and tipped the milk over the formidable Italian head teacher. There was stunned silence. For a split second I stayed very still while raising my eyebrows at the head teacher.

Then, without missing a beat, I became a fumbling 'English gentleman' teacher again. 'So sorry,' I said, rubbing the milk further into her clothes. 'How clumsy of me. Your poor clothes are ruined.' I looked at the Italian staff again, nodded my head, then went back to my seat. Every Italian staff member and pupil knew what had happened. The English head (whose employ I was in) and staff, however, were seated behind me at the opposite end of the room and would not have seen my expression or raised eyebrows. Nor did they know of the fling, so they believed the spilt milk to be an accident. When I came up for a dismissal hearing, they threatened to walk out of the school, and thus saved me my job. But even if I had lost my job over it, it would have been worth it.

The head teacher reacted by calling the overall boss of the entire chain of foreign language schools to Oxford. There was some irony here for us both. Last time I saw her she was interviewing me for this job and inviting me up to her hotel room for a 'drink', even though the interview took place in the hotel's extremely well-stocked bar. That's unpaid prostitution in my book: it's using sex to get something, only no actual money changes hands. In escorting terms, it's what is called trading up. That's fine as long as both parties are happy, and I would have gone to her room too – she was attractive, I wanted the job and a bit of extra protection in the system never hurts – but I already had a date waiting for me in the hotel lobby.

There was always a date waiting for me in the lobby at this time. Who knew then that that's what I would become: a date, hurrying through a thousand hotel lobbies. But at that time, this was my life, whether in Oxford, London or, once the summer in England was over, Barcelona. It was girls, drinking, teaching, weight-training and long-distance running. When I was in Spain I was great at drumming up business for the school, but, exhausted from the constant effort of covering up and coping with my dyslexia, didn't manage to learn much Spanish. As usual since leaving the church, I felt like an outsider; not quite in the swing of things. That's why, when I return from Barcelona, neither richer nor more enlightened, I do what all those with one degree, a TEFL certificate, eighteen months' worth of teaching experience and still no idea what to make of their life do: I go back to Anglia Ruskin in Cambridge to do a master's degree. What do I choose for my subject? Christian History.

Not that I spent much time studying. Instead I trained, kept fit and partied, all in equal measure. I did things on the spur of the moment too, because my two supposed main occupations – my degree and the job I got in a café making sandwiches – made me feel like the living dead. Because here's the thing. If I wasn't thinking much about religion and history, I was still doing a lot of thinking and several pennies were dropping, and hard. I remembered a friend of mine doing a talk at a school assembly years before and quoting a survey which said that when retired people were asked what they'd do if they could relive their life, the most popular theme of answer was: *take more risks*. That struck me at the time, but during my first few months back in Cambridge the words came ringing back. I thought: I don't want to live a life of regret. I don't want to get stuck doing a boring job living the quiet life of my parents. That way may be absolutely right for them but I already knew it was absolutely wrong for me. The more I thought about what I didn't want for my life, the more the life of an escort seemed to be the one I wanted. I even drew a graph to help me clarify my thinking.

From the age of nought to eighteen you are dependent on your parents or others. Your physical strength is growing but you have no financial freedom. If you're lucky enough to go to university you've by now got total physical strength and hopefully are in good health, but you are still, if you are a normal student, constrained financially. That begins to change when you graduate, or should do, so that from the ages of twenty-two to fifty-seven-ish you have increasing amounts of money, and good health. Let's even give it another ten years, and assume your mental and physical abilities stay pretty sharp till your mid-sixties. After that, you may well have more money than you've ever had before, because you haven't retired yet, but it's more than likely that your health will be in some kind of decline.

Even if you remain fit and well, there's no getting round the fact that the forty-five years in the middle of your life are your prime years. Only, what are we doing with the *daylight hours* of pretty much any one of those given days over the entire forty-five years? *Working*. It seems to me that among my friends even the most dedicated father spends more time at the office – often a lot more time – than with his kids.

My goals were both to become financially secure and to break this routine, which meant, I reasoned, doing anything I could to serve this purpose. I had read something that had a profound effect on me about Alexander the Great conquering Asia. He said that he'd been able to do it because the people there hadn't learnt to pronounce the word 'no'. I had given my life to the Church with innocence, naivety and purity and where had it got me? I had emerged lost and confused, but I thought: I'm going to take back what is mine. Some people find nobility in being poor and thrifty, but not me. For me, I think there is integrity in saying, if you can: you've got it, I'm going to get it too. The rules aren't fair, so I'm going to bend them to my will. I can't change a system that favours those who have over those who don't, but I can make sure I'm OK.

I looked out of the window of the café where I was working and realized that the parking meter was on a better hourly rate than me. It had been almost two years since I placed that disastrous first escorting ad in my local paper. In November of 1998 I was ready to try again.

The first job didn't go brilliantly. As soon as I decided I was going to give it another shot, I put an ad in a local Cambridge newspaper and only received one call – *from a man*. Now, I was expecting that, after the amount of calls from men I'd received two years earlier in response to my first ad, and the truth is that any male escort who claims that he doesn't do 'gay for pay' (and it doesn't matter how straight he is) is almost certainly lying. I knew that even though I am totally straight I was going to have to accept men as clients, but I wasn't ready to do it so soon. Nor is this, as the title of this book implies, the focus of the story I'm telling here. I knew my phone wouldn't be flooded with calls from women, but I was confused by the lack of any calls but one. On closer examination of the ad, I realized the newspaper had printed the last digit of my number wrong. That meant the guy must have dialled and redialled a ridiculous number of times with different numbers trying to find me. How many people, I wondered, had dialled the wrong number just once and quite reasonably given up.

A week later the ad came out correctly. Within minutes my phone was on fire. I accepted the first job that came from a woman and so my escorting career, proper, began. Still, there is no doubt I was a novice. The wrong phone number in the newspaper was not my only mistake as I started my new career. The woman who called and booked me for my first appointment turned out to be a thin, untalkative, rather formal manager for Vodafone, probably in her early forties. Mostly I remember that she lived bloody hours from anywhere. I had to get a train out of Cambridge and we then drove for miles into the countryside to get to her house. That's a big mistake in escorting. You don't allow yourself to be led by a stranger to some place out in the middle of nowhere with no way of getting home if things go pear-shaped.

Plus, I didn't charge her for any travel time, so although the actual escorting work was pretty straightforward and didn't take long, all in all it added up to several hours out of my day for a £50 payment (a figure I more or less plucked out of thin air, as I still had no idea what to charge), which she tried to bargain down when we talked on the phone. At least I managed to stay firm on that front. Another escorting lesson: your price is not negotiable. Period. Unless you decide to put it up. Lesson three: charge for your travel. Train fares and taxi rides? The client pays for those. And of course you always take a taxi, even if you live five minutes from your destination. You'll have that, along with the money for the return journey, and your fee, up front, please, you say politely but firmly, no ifs or buts or games.

The Thin Woman picked me up from the train station and we drove to her house in virtual silence. I attempted some small talk, but gave up when she replied in mono-syllables. Was she nervous? As she kept her gaze so firmly on the road, I took the opportunity to study her gaunt profile, her long, quite beautiful neck, the veins that stood up on the backs of her ringless hands. She didn't betray the slightest hint of emotion. I, on the other hand, was nervous. If all went to plan, this would be the first time I had been paid for sex, but the memory of the disastrous time with the two police officers weighed heavy on my mind.

We pulled up in front of a nondescript house and got out of the car and she let us into her place. I placed a hand on the small of her back as we walked towards her front door, but there was something in her stiff posture that made me drop my hand. Was she going to be that controlled in the bedroom?

'Nice place,' I said, as she let me in. And it was – but in a tastefully decorated, showhome kind of sense. There wasn't much on display that showed her personality, few books, no photos or artwork.

She smiled tightly at me, and I followed her into her kitchen, which was white, immaculately clean and looked as if she didn't cook there much. She took two glasses from a cupboard and poured us some wine. I took a sip, while she knocked hers back. I felt something curl round my leg and looked down. It was a cat, a grey one with dark green eyes. I reached down and scratched the cat's head.

The Thin Woman smiled. 'That's Sheba,' she said. 'She's a bit of a flirt.'

It was the most she had said to me since I got in her car. Suddenly I had a clear idea of who this woman was and why she needed to hire an escort. She was the cliché of the unmarried, professional woman who, finding herself in her forties with only a cat for company, realizes that she's probably going to be alone for the rest of her life. And the sad thing was that this woman probably knew that she was a cliché, and understood that the choices she had made in her life had led her to this solitary existence. Perhaps she was happy with those choices 90 per cent of the time. But then there was that 10 per cent when she needed to be with someone, needed to be touched.

I suddenly felt less nervous. It was obvious what I needed to do – I needed to make her feel less lonely, if only for a short amount of time. I placed my hand on her arm gently, and slid it along her back to her shoulder, trying to pull her into an embrace.

'I'm sorry,' she said. 'I'm not really into kissing or cuddling.'

'That's fine,' I said softly, 'whatever you want. I'm here for you.'

She swiftly glanced at me, as if to check that I was being serious, and then took her glass of wine and finished it.

'My bedroom's upstairs and on the left,' she told me.

'The bathroom is opposite it. Get undressed in the bath-room and I'll see you there.'

So, that's it, then. We're going to get right down to it. I took off everything apart from my boxer shorts and waited for a few moments to mentally prepare myself and to give the Thin Woman time to change. There wasn't very much that was sexy about this situation, but I knew, from that farcical experience with the police officers, that it wasn't about what I felt, it was about her, and what she wanted.

After what seemed like an appropriate interval, I left the bathroom and went to the door of her room. It was slightly ajar, but looked dark inside. I tapped the door with my knuckle and pushed it open when I heard her say, 'Come in.' She was lying on the bed, naked, her back against the headboard. The light from the hallway made her look vulnerable, a little younger. She had a good body and, if a little wiry for my tastes, obviously kept herself in shape.

I went to the side of the bed and sat down. She touched my shoulder and ran her hand down my chest. I could feel my body responding, more to the thought that I was being paid for what I was about to do than the situation itself. Her breasts were small but well shaped. I ran my hand over them, rubbing her nipples with the side of my thumb and she sighed. 'You have beautiful breasts,' I said, taking one of her nipples into my mouth.

I was hard now, so when she pulled down my boxer shorts, I had no worries that she would be disappointed.

She lay down on her back, and I leaned over her. 'What do you want?' I asked her as I nuzzled her neck.

'I want,' she said as I ran my hand down her thigh. 'I want you to put this on.'

She had placed a condom on the bed beside her.

'You don't want me to—'

'No,' she interrupted firmly. 'I just want you to fuck me. That's it.'

And that really was it. She wanted hardly any foreplay at all. I put the condom on and I fucked her. She seemed to enjoy it – but as she made hardly any noise, or spoke, it was difficult to tell – and just as I was about to come she pushed her nails into my back.

Afterwards she called a cab to take me back to the station, which I paid for using the fifty pounds I had earned.

On the train back home I thought about the evening. I didn't feel damaged or used or abused or manipulated. It wasn't a mindblowing experience, but for someone's first real attempt at being an escort it could have been a whole lot worse, as I knew too well. This time I didn't panic, didn't feel thrown and certainly felt no shame. I had done everything the Thin Woman had wanted me to do, and I think that she enjoyed it. The customer, I thought to myself, may not always be right, but they are when it comes to what they want for their money. But then again, it did seem that I was very much still a novice, and that I needed to do some research into my new trade. For starters, I realized that I needed to address the time it took going to and from appointments and factor that into my price. I was annoyed with myself that I hadn't thought about that when I told Thin Woman what I charged. I decided that I wouldn't let myself be so unprepared again.

Finding out what price the market would support me charging seemed like a good place to start, and so I did my own ringing round to start to get some ideas. Fifty pounds for an hour's work, I discovered, was ridiculously below market price. Plus, every time I got off the phone I had several messages from potential clients waiting for me. The business, I quickly realized, was out there and money could potentially be made.

The cliché is that escorting is work for the down-trodden. That it is some kind of desperate measure, and that choosing it results in a whole range of negatives. Not for me, nor for many I know. Almost immediately, escorting was the opposite of the last resort. For the first time since leaving the Church, I felt like I had escaped metaphorical financial captivity. Plus, I discovered I liked 'the life'. A lot of escorts do. There is something wonderful about being fancied and being the fulfilment of someone's fantasy. There is also something wonderful about being handed dirty, filthy, wonderful cash.

My first clients who called me on that crisp, cold, sunny November day were, I came to realize, typical of the kind of people who would be attracted to an escort like me – a straight-looking and -sounding, respectable, educated student. I advertised myself as a student, and the rest was easy enough to discern over the telephone.

In the early days my first clients were mostly sympathetic to any nervousness because, after all, there is no escorting helpline you can ring up for advice; no apprenticeship scheme or manual to turn to; no one flashing PowerPoint presentations on 'The Best and Most Profitable Way Forward'.

Still, I was a quick learner. And I had a few things in my favour. I may have been a student, but I wasn't living in student digs or sharing a flat with friends. Instead, I had rented a room in a house right in the centre of Cambridge, owned and lived in by an elderly French woman I simply (and ironically) called Madame, who was in her late nineties. Not that she encouraged visitors of any kind. Girls were banned, she told me, and I thought better than to ask about clients. Luckily she was deaf and so sneaking visitors in and up the stairs to my digs at the back of the house was easy enough, and the sneaky factor mostly added to my clients' fantasy about me, a straight Cambridge student, living in digs and earning money to fund my further forays into academia. I didn't bother to give specifics as to which university I was at and most people tended to assume it was the 'big' one. With an accent like mine, the fantasy held. I was happy enough to encourage the carefree image of a student on a bicycle getting up to no good in the attic of his elderly French landlady, while in reality beginning to learn fast about offshore accounts, stock market bonds and safety deposit boxes.

CHAPTER 4

Secure Your Future

When you start out as an escort the world is all over you. Everybody, it seemed, wanted to check out the new boy, and in Cambridge not only was I new, I was unique. In 1998 I was the *only* male escort in Cambridge. My phone rang off the hook and no wonder: I had no competition at all for some years. And when someone else did finally cotton on to the Cambridge gold rush, it didn't make much difference. The newcomer was much older than me and used the same name as I was using at that time: Richard. It's quite common in escorting to pinch someone else's name when you start up. It's an easy way of poaching some of their business. I didn't really care. There was enough business for both of us and my clients didn't remain confused for long. One of them, after he had been to see him, told me that his real name was Andrew, so I started to place a few ads using that name, which is, as you'll have noticed, the one that I use to this day. That rattled him. Especially as his day job was in an area of the civil service that wouldn't appreciate his moonlighting activities, and which a local paper would eat up with a spoon, as they would the fact that he was also a diligent school governor of the school his child attended.

Both of us, of course, claimed to be five years younger. That's standard in a business like escorting, where youth is usually a premium. You can still get work, though, when you get older. Remember when Max Mosley got busted? The dominatrices he was seeing weren't exactly young and beautiful, but they were apparently good escorts with a dungeon in Chelsea, where rent costs the earth. Max Mosley would have been paying top dollar and presumably, until he was set up, he felt he was getting value for money.

There is a guy who works in Central London called Brian who is in his seventies and pretty tubby. But he's never short of a job. Far from it: Brian's a legend in the escorting world and everyone knows him. He specializes in spanking. A lot of his business is from younger people (that's pretty much everyone for Brian) who find April–November relationships (the term used for younger adults who fancy older people) sexy. Some people like age, others might go for very hairy men. It's something to do with them wanting a *real* man to hold them. But then for some men and many women hair on the back is a huge turn-off. What can you do? You can never be all things to all people, but being a good escort means having good interpersonal skills. It's no coincidence that female prostitutes in the seventeenth century were referred to as actresses.

For the record, I have very little body hair. Most escorts have tried a bit of shaving here and there, but, as with everything else to do with the body, what is adored by one person may be a turn-off for someone else. Some people think too much shaving makes you look like a porn star, and some clients are turned on by that, but an equal amount find it unappealing. So you have to do what *you* feel like doing and what is going to make you feel good.

Everyone wants something different and so you have to decide what you are comfortable doing for clients and where to set your boundaries. Mostly, you have to learn as you go along, because there is no one really there, especially at the beginning, to give you advice.

Well, that's not strictly true. After a few months, I received a call from Nikki, a female escort asking me whether I did 'duos'. I said I did, and we quickly set up a date to do a job together with a client of hers who wanted to watch her getting fucked. I remember thinking, on my way to her house: I'm going to meet a prostitute. I was intrigued as to what both she and her flat would be like, and I suppose part of me wondered if it wouldn't be some kind of lewd boudoir lit by a red light bulb with scarves draped all over the place.

The reality was much different to my imagination. Nikki was a black woman in her late twenties, very attractive with amazingly beautiful eyes. I was immediately attracted to her, and thought it was reciprocal. She was from the north of Africa and had a practical, no-nonsense manner about her that I liked. And her rooms? Not much different to mine, I thought as I took a look round her flat.

'Now,' she said, 'a few things before this guy comes around. Firstly, he just likes to watch, but he doesn't like thinking that you're watching him, so don't look in his direction. He'll sit over there,' she pointed to an armchair that I was sure I had seen in Habitat, 'so we need to position ourselves,' she indicated an area of the bed, 'here. He may come for a closer look, but he won't get involved or anything, so if he does don't worry, just ignore him and concentrate on me.'

'Fine,' I said. It all seemed straightforward to me. 'What about foreplay?'

Nikki shrugged. 'He likes to see a bit of that but I'm not too fussed, to be honest.'

The doorbell rang. 'That's him,' she said needlessly, 'stay here,' and I waited nervously in the bedroom. I could hear Nikki opening the door, greeting her client – unlike me who tries to engage and charm my clients and seduce them with flattery, she was brisk and businesslike – and soon the door opened to reveal a balding, middle-aged man with glasses. You couldn't tell from his clothes if he was a businessman or a builder – he was dressed casually but smartly. The expression on his face was part embarrassment, part excitement. Nikki showed him to his chair and he sat down.

'Right then, shall we get comfortable,' Nikki said, and started peeling off her clothes.

I followed suit and soon Nikki and I were rolling around on her bed naked. It was odd, here we were, having sex, pretending that the reason for us having sex – the man in the corner – wasn't there. Rather than ignoring the elephant in the room, we were ignoring the voyeur. I went down on Nikki and almost immediately she started moaning – purely for the man's benefit of course, because I could tell she wasn't as turned on as her groans would have you believe. Underneath her sighs I heard the sound of a zipper being pulled down, and the atmosphere changed in the room again.

I can't pretend that the situation wasn't weird – I was pleasuring someone who didn't care to be pleasured for the sake of this anonymous guy's pleasure – and yet, I was kind of getting a kick out of it. There's something powerful about being the focus of someone's erotic gaze.

With a great deal of noise Nikki pretended to come – I could hear the guy's breathing become faster and shallower – rolled me over and went down on me, expertly putting on a condom on me with her mouth. I was just starting to get into it when she stopped giving me a blow-job, lowered herself on to me and we started having sex. I heard the creak of a chair and was about to look round when Nikki took my face in her hands and directed my eyes back towards hers.

It was all over soon after that. We were done, and the anonymous man saw, came and left. Nikki quickly dressed herself in a robe and followed him out. When she came back, she had a roll of cash with her. 'You are green, aren't you? Here,' she said, peeling off some notes and handing them to me. 'You should have asked me for the money up front. You should always ask for the money up front,' she tutted.

I took the cash. It was easily four times the amount I usually charged.

'Is this right?' I said.

'Yes. Why?' Nikki's face looked perturbed. 'How much do you normally charge?'

I told her and she snorted. 'You have to quadruple your rates or you'll price other people out of the market. God, you're so green.'

I got dressed, pushing the notes that Nikki gave me into the back pocket of my jeans. Nikki was clearing up some tissues on the dresser. There was something that I wanted to ask her, but it felt weird. This, after all, was my first time with a professional. 'So, how was it, anyway?'

Nikki turned to face me, an indulgent smile on her face. 'It was fine,' she assured me. 'And I'll use you again, no problem. In fact,' she said with a saucy smile, 'there's some other things I could teach you as well.'

I left the house feeling at once slightly out of my comfort zone and strangely elated. But at last I had learnt something. At this point in my career I was learning something all the time. I still am.

Increasing my rates didn't affect my business at all. I was getting more and more calls. The thing about being the only male escort (this was before Richard turned up) in a medium-size provincial town which is home to one of the best universities in the world is that you get all sorts of customers. I felt a bit like a country doctor or a vet like you see in one of the Sunday-night TV series: like them, I was called out by people from every slice of the community. If you are an escort in Chelsea, London, then most of your clients are going to be relatively rich. But in a place like Cambridge I saw all sorts of people from every walk of life, from students to business people, high-street retailers to academics. I think that's one of the things that surprised me most: my clients aren't weirdoes or perverts or some strange, segregated section of society. They are just ordinary people on the whole who are either willing, or actively wanting, to pay for sexual exploration or just to have a bit of fun.

Of course it's better to get sexual stuff from a loving, intimate relationship, but some people don't have the luxury of that. For whatever reason they can't manage it or don't want to. And to go without any sex at all is to exist in a parched place. At least if you go to an escort, you are getting something. It may be second best in my view (though frequently this is not the view of the client), but it's something. Personally, the thought of paying a counsellor a pound a minute to listen to my emotional problems isn't my ideal scenario. I'd rather talk to an understanding and loyal close friend who knows me well and understands the context of where I'm coming from, and whose advice I should listen to because I know them, rather than paying a professional, but not everyone's so lucky. And sometimes it's not even as complicated as that. Sometimes people hire me just because they want a bit of fun and a lot of sex.

Picture the scene. The halls of residence of a good second-tier university. Concrete breeze blocks with narrow rooms off long corridors; girls on one side, boys on the other. Toilets and shower rooms at either end, together with a shared kitchen of skank. Everywhere, even on fine days, there is a slight smell of mould or clothes that have never been dried properly, plus of course traces of BO and pee, fried food, dirty laundry, toilets, cigarettes, marijuana and cheese and onion crisps.

I was there after I received a call from a girl, a student at the university, who has ordered in, not a pizza, but an escort, to her small room in one of these corridors. When

I'd received the call I'd wondered if it was a joke. She quickly passed through my trouble-spotting metaphorical telephone grid because she sounded like a normal, nice woman interested in experimenting, but when she told me her address: room J22 or whatever it was, in the very halls of residence whose gym I used daily, I wondered if it was a prank. Sometimes you get that: a bunch of female students call you up and ask what size your dick is, or try and get you to turn up at the rooms of one of their unsuspecting girlfriends.

After a while this sort of call no longer passed through my grid, as a prank caller will inevitably either ask the 'wrong' questions or simply feel wrong. Every escort learns over time how to quickly differentiate between real business and joke phone calls. Learning to both hone and listen to your instinct becomes second nature for every good escort. For most people, calling up an escort is no laughing matter. Nor was it for this woman, and so I took my chances and found my way to her corridor. But it did make me wonder if what I was doing was madness because all I could think was: oh shit, I'm in student halls, am I going to get into trouble here? What if someone said rape? What could I say to defend myself, a strange man going to see a woman? If something went down, who is anyone going to listen to? But nothing went down, almost literally.

The girl who opened her door to me was very beautiful and made-up, with perfect nails and deliberately messy just-got-out-of-bed blonde hair. The first time I went to see her, and I saw her over a number of weeks, she was wearing red hot pants. She became Baywatch Girl in my mind and in my mobile phone's address book (every client has something by their name in an escort's phone, to help them identify who they are or what they are into) and the name was apt.

When I first saw her I thought: wow. The dream client, even if her single bed is tiny and attached to the wall on two sides. She was beautiful and clever and dithery all at once, and she clearly came from money. She may have been living in student digs but Daddy's trust fund paid for the huge amounts of clearly expensive clothes and shoes that spilt out all over the floor. She told me she didn't drink and I could see from the mass of books and papers that she took her studies seriously, and yet there she was, about to peel off her hot pants after paying me over two hundred pounds to have sex with her. Just in case all this wasn't enough, I couldn't help but notice that she had a great bum. And if you can divide straight men into bum-men and tit-men I'm a bit of a bum-man. Could it have got any better? Well, yes, it could. Sadly, though, it didn't and the reality was that having sex with this Baywatch Girl was like having sex with a block of wood.

Was Baywatch Girl shy or embarrassed about having sex with an escort or just plain having sex? The honest answer is I don't know what was going on because normally when you are having sex with someone there is a certain warmth between you or some signal that they are enjoying it, or not enjoying it quite enough yet, so you sense that you should change what you're doing – something at least, *some response*. But with Baywatch Girl I got no indication of *anything at all* from her.

When we kissed, it was as if *I* were kissing *her*, a wax work, rather than two people kissing one another. When I went down on her she lay like a plank of wood and not one cell of her body moved an inch. At each point I asked her if what I was doing was OK; if I should kiss her, if I should go down on her and to each question she nodded her head. When I said: 'Shall I put a condom on? Do you want to have sex?' she said yes. And so I entered her in this narrow student single bed. But the bed was the most comfortable part of the situation. I never thought that sleeping with a beautiful woman could be so weird, but it was.

I wanted to say to her: 'I don't know if you know I am even here. *And I am inside you.*' I don't know if she didn't know what she was doing or she didn't know how to have sex or she didn't know if she wanted to have sex or if all of these things were the reason she had called an escort. What I did know was that something unhappy was going on. I wished I could ask her if there was something in her past that prevented her from fully participating in sex, but although we had been physically intimate, we weren't emotionally intimate and I still wasn't sure what sort of boundaries I should maintain between my clients and me. As I was cycling home I kept thinking: how unusual, how strange, what to make of it? And there is no one you can talk to about such an experience; no one to tell as no one knew I was doing escort work. That is the trouble with being an escort – the law forbids you to work with more than one person in a house. In terms of safety, this makes escort work dangerous if there's no one in the same house as you to help should you be attacked by a client. But also it makes your life isolating if there's no one at home with whom you can share what's happened in your day or ask advice. Although you're surrounded by people, as an escort you're often very isolated.

Baywatch Girl wasn't my only student client at that time. At around the same time I was called by a post-graduate studying for her PhD at Cambridge University. She was only three or four years older than Baywatch, probably about twenty-four, but she seemed like she came from a different generation, an Edwardian one perhaps. She had the look and feel of academia imprinted all over her. You could tell she had an incredibly well-fed mind, but in many other ways she seemed somewhat lonely. She lived in a shared house – picture trying to pass the clutter of bikes in the hall without tripping up; try finding a clean mug for a cup of tea – clearly on a pittance, not a penny of which she spent on her appearance as far as I could tell. She was plain-looking, though not ugly, and she wore glasses, which of course hung on a chain round her neck (I repeat, she was only twenty-four) when they weren't on her nose. She was quite up front about why she called me. Though she was lecturing already and teaching, she wasn't yet an actual lecturer. But neither was she any longer quite a student, and she said she found that somehow sex was eluding her. I suggested with a smile that getting out of the university library might help, but she protested, saying that she'd had some of her best sex in libraries! She said she saw no shame in calling an escort (I hadn't asked if she did), but was just glad she found an ad for one so easily. I joked that it was good to see her investing her student loan so wisely.

'You know, Andrew,' she said, 'academia is not *so* far away from what you're doing.' I asked her what she meant.

'Well,' she explained, 'to get anywhere, academics write endless articles that they're not necessarily passionate about and which aren't always especially original, but they do it just so that they can get them published. It means the department gets a better star rating, which means more grant money.' I chuckled at her comparison. It did sound oddly familiar. 'That's not the only thing,' she continued. 'Because if you're an academic who doesn't get work published, don't hold out for a promotion, no matter how good a teacher you are. So in many ways, we're all prostituting our talents.' Then she took off her glasses. 'Come over here,' she said smiling and beginning to undress me before hopping into bed and pulling the covers up over her body, a gesture I found charming and sweet, never mind that it was also necessary as the room was freezing.

I felt curiously turned on by this plain-looking girl hidden under her multiple blankets, and for all Baywatch's beauty, for all her neat little bum in its red hot pants, it was PhD girl, so full of warmth and response, that I loved fucking. (Nor does it surprise me to learn that she is now a professor.)

For if success in academia is all about intellectual curiosity, to be a good lover you need to have sexual curiosity, and PhD girl had that in abundance. For example, she once bought an antique academic cane from eBay and asked me to use it on her. Underneath all those clothes she had a pert little bottom and the thought of spanking her with it was exciting, although she warned me, once again, that we had to try and be quiet because she didn't want to disturb her housemates or let them know what we were up to. But the sound of a thwack on bare skin is not really one that you can hush up. It only took a couple of whacks before I noticed that she was shaking with suppressed laughter. And once she started giggling, I started giggling too, and we ended up under the covers, our hands over each other's mouths, as we fucked each other senseless. After we finished she said that she had never quite understood why some people were turned on by spanking, and she'd thought she'd try it, just to see.

It wasn't all about fucking though. All in all, I was living. For the first time in years I felt utterly alive. I was busy from morning to night. If I wasn't with a client then I was at the gym, though never a gym in the basement of a building because God forbid my phone would ever be out of range. My phone rang incessantly and phone calls meant business and business meant money. Business also often, though not always, meant good times. Like hanging out with Antiquity Woman.

Antiquity Woman was a fabulous client, ideal in about eight thousand ways. Antiquity Woman loved to surround herself with beautiful things, and she herself was a sensual type of person. Perhaps that's why she hired me – she loved having a beautiful boy – as she called me – available to do her bidding. Her one irritating quality was that she always wanted more – not in an aggressive, arrogant, assuming way, but rather in a laid-back, dope-smoking, well-off, philosophical, these-things-are-inevitable, Canadian way, which wasn't that surprising because that's what she was: a laid-back, well-off, intellectual Canadian dope smoker who looked like she'd just stepped out of a Hollywood movie set on a northern Californian campus. Antiquity Woman had a large Georgian town house in the best bit of Cambridge. She was a distinguished art historian and academic who traded antiquities in Zurich. She kept a good many too: her house was chock-a-block with two-, three- and four-thousand-year-old objects.

To get to her sitting room you had to walk through mini corridors of books piled into towers along the hallway. Pictures hung everywhere. Every piece of furniture was a fabulous antique. You'd be having a pee and what's that there on the bathroom counter glimmering away? Oh, only a piece of Byzantine pottery. Antiquity Woman seemed to like a lot of everything. She quickly became a regular client, and by regular I mean twice a week. I got to know her very well, and one of her most marked characteristics was her generosity. She gave me an extra set of keys to her house because she spent most of her time in London, New York, or in Zurich where she had an even grander house filled with even older treasures.

I used to water her plants, yes, and she knew that sometimes I'd stay overnight. That was fine by her. I should think that servicing clients in her bed and having sixteen of my football mates to stay during a stag weekend would have been less what she had in mind, but never mind, what she didn't know, I reasoned, didn't hurt her. Only she did find out, of course. Sixteen pissed footie boys moved a set of Corinthian column heads out of the way with military precision then slept all over her floor, head to tail, like sardines, without disturbing even a speck of dust. But Baywatch Girl? She only left strands of her blonde hair all over Antiquity Woman's art deco bathtub.

And while Antiquity Woman was laid-back about most things in life, including me having other clients, she got curiously jealous when I told her about anyone too young or too beautiful (she was probably in her late fifties herself). Blonde hair in the bathtub (plus most of her gin drunk) meant I had the front-door keys taken off me for a bit as punishment. I guess I should have felt guilty for abusing her generosity, but there was a part of me that felt entitled to such luxury that I never did. And Antiquity Woman treated my misdemeanours as no more than youthful indiscretions, punishing me no more than you would a wayward puppy, so no wonder I took advantage of her hospitality.

One afternoon when I was at Antiquity's house (she being away), a new client phoned me up and asked for an overnight session that night. She said she'd have to leave early in the morning, which suited me fine because I had to get up early too and actually make it to a lecture for once. I gave her Antiquity's address and I remember her arriving and asking if she could pay by credit card. I suppose the set-up at the house seemed eccentric enough that I might just. But no, I told her, cash only, and so she marched off to the cash point before our 'night of passion' could begin. You could say I was surprised when, after she left the next morning, a few minutes before me, I saw her again in the lecture hall, the guest speaker on some aspect of religious history at the lecture I was so assiduously attending. I can't put into words what her face looked like when ten minutes into the lecture she saw me sitting in the third row and realized who I was. After the lecture I made a point of asking her a question about her subject (so that she knew I was a bona-fide student and not some weird stalker escort) and at the same time took the opportunity to reassure her that I'd never give a client away. There's a universal rule in this business, because part of what people are paying for is discretion, and it would be to break a semi-sacred contract to abuse that implicit trust.

I was inspired by Antiquity Woman and her success and her beautiful house, which I knew to be one of several she owned, and I decided quickly that I wanted to build a very real future for myself, and that the best way to do that was to save my money and invest it wisely. There is a cliché about high-class escorts frittering away their money on short-term luxuries: designer clothes, handbags and shoes, perfect highlights and cocaine. I'm sure there is some truth in this, but not for me. I may have been earning good money quickly but that was not how I was going to spend it. I made sure I paid special attention to Antiquity Woman's tax arrangements and investments.

I drew up a plan. I was very specific. I drew a picture of a house I had seen in Cambridge and wanted to buy. I divided the drawing into 110 squares because the house cost £110,000. Every time I cleared a thousand pounds – and because my rent was cheap and I ate most of my meals and drank most of my drinks courtesy of my clients I didn't have many outgoings – I'd pay off a square of mortgage. My goal was to buy the entire house outright in my first year as an escort. After that, I decided, I'd see what would happen. But I wanted a house, and all that that stood for – security, comfort, an asset, a home of my own – and escorting seemed the quickest and easiest way to get one. No, more than that, it seemed the only way to me at that time to get one. Though I have long since sold that first house, I still have that first drawing. When I look at it I am reminded of so many things, not least my first year of escorting and its accompanying sentimental education.

All In A Day's Work In The Ugly Lovely Business

A typical day, such as it existed, in my life as a male escort was marked by one constant, regular thing: my phones. I have two phones and five extra lines for diverting calls and they ring all the time. Most people's working lives are dominated by office hours or deadlines; mine is ruled by my mobile phones. Here's how I see it: the phone is on twenty-four hours a day, and should be answered twenty-four hours a day. People mostly find my number through my advertisements, and, when I started running them (in about 2000), my websites. I keep my ads simple and change them a little according to the publication I am using, which I soon no longer limited to local newspapers. Even when I was based in Cambridge, I was happy to do an overnight in London, Birmingham or abroad if the money was right, and sometimes out-of-town clients, who spotted me in a London paper, would be coming to Cambridge or near enough for some reason and want to perk up their trip.

Jobs come up all the time, which means that if you can be bothered to go to all the jobs you are offered, even at 4 a.m., you can make a lot of money. I was willing. My feeling was, if I'm going to do this, I might as well do it properly; if I'm going to bother putting an advert in a listings magazine I might as well maximize that advert. I probably spend about £1000 each month on advertising, so I have to make sure the ads work for me and earn their keep. That's £1000 cash. You just go in to the office with your cash, place your ad and it runs, no questions asked. There is usually no problem at all with this, as all publications know what you are selling, but some feign a check of some kind, like asking for a personal trainer/massage certificate. They never study them too carefully though.

The phone is not just your best business tool; it can also be something of a torment. If you're hiding the fact that you're an escort from your friends and family, and most people are, then you can't take calls in front of them. You have to make sure you're not overheard. I don't know quite how I'd explain to one of the football boys if he overheard me saying into the phone: 'I'm just under six foot, muscular, with an athletic build, tanned smooth skin, deep blue eyes, blond hair, seven inches down below, uncut.' So you get good at constantly darting out of the door and speaking in code on the phone. When I began to buy houses to rent, as I soon did, I blamed the constant calls on my property business – it's always good to have a cover story handy.

Mine, before my housing business started, developed somewhat out of my control and as much as it irritated me, it did at least stop people asking questions, and the fewer questions asked, the fewer lies I had to tell. Remember, it wasn't long since I had been a committed Christian and had lived my life in a mostly truthful way. I had to learn to lie quickly, because as an escort lying is something you have to do all the time – from using a different name to saying that you are 'enjoying this too'. One thing I learnt is that a half truth is much easier to maintain than a total lie.

A big part of my life at this time was dedicated to the gym and keeping fit. I was Mr Muscle Man and so it was easy for me to say that I earned money while I was doing my masters degree working as a security guard for high-class escorts, though as you can imagine I kept it pretty vague. That was just about acceptable to a close group of friends – the protective role always leavens anything potentially unseemly – while still being edgy enough for them not to ask too many questions about it. It also explained my high volumes of phone calls and the fact I always answered them in private.

If it was assumed at first that my role in 'security' would be temporary, then after a couple of years with nothing seeming to change except the fact that I was no longer studying, my brother and friends concluded that it obviously suited me, and knowing that I wouldn't settle for taking orders for too long, imagined that I must have some kind of organizational role. In other words, although it was never said out loud, the story was I worked as an agency organizer. It once came up when my brother and a group of us were all drunk together and I neither denied nor confirmed it. Because to deny it meant I would have to come up with another explanation and I didn't have one of those, or at least not one that would be accompanied by such a blanket 'don't ask, don't tell, don't try and find out' policy. I had to strategically leak the idea that I was a pimp one drunken night at my brother's university when my phone was stolen and text messages that might have been read would have needed some explanation.

As an escort I carry two phones with me all the time, one for work and one for my personal life, and no, I don't ever get confused between the two. They look different for a start, and you don't get confused if you answer a phone and someone asks if they have reached Robert or Mathew or one of the other professional names I use. If the phone is never off, it is also never out of range. As well as not going to underground gyms, you learn not to go to restaurants in the basements of buildings or indeed into the underground itself, because if you're out of range, you've lost business.

Of course not all callers will make good or even accept-able customers, and the first thing you want to do is filter out any dangerous ones or bad payers. That's why a phone call is essential, rather than operating your business purely via email. It's only by listening to someone's voice and their phone manner that you are able to pick up on some of the key signs that enables you to filter out the no-goes. A caller who tries to barter my price down is a very bad sign. So is someone who wants endless descriptions of what I 'do' or what I look like: often these people don't intend to book an appointment at all, but are just using the phone call itself to get off in some way.

Callers who book me a long time in advance – and particularly those who won't give me their phone number for confirmation purposes (obviously I explain how discreet I am) become low priority. More often than not they then cancel or just don't show up. You also *never* give out your address over the phone when someone is booking an appointment. Instead, I tell clients to come to the street next to mine, call me from there and then I give them specific instructions. There was even a handy working phone box on my street if they felt uncomfortable calling me from a mobile. It just means I'm not giving out my address to all and sundry. Serious customers who follow through, yes, but idle callers, no. You don't want odd bods, weirdoes, stalkers having your address, and there are a lot of weirdoes out there who enjoy calling escorts.

I had a stalker once, and though she didn't actually frighten me (though I imagine if you reverse our sexes then the whole story would seem more sinister), she did stress me out. Judith was a woman in her early twenties who was both prim and wild. By that I mean she had an ultra respectable job in the civil service and she wore smart suits every day, but she also had many outlandish tattoos concealed beneath her clothes and was willing to call up an escort (perhaps several, who knows?) and pay for sex for the thrill of it. She also wore, all the time as far as I could tell, copious amounts of perfume, one that had a very distinctive smell. So far, so good (except that to this day I can't stand the smell of that particular scent).

The problem was that she became infatuated with me and started to behave like a teenager with a crush she could not keep under control. I became, I think, an obsession for Judith. This manifested itself in several ways. She would call me up incessantly, often just wanting to talk rather than book an appointment. She always wanted our sessions to go over time. I began receiving anonymously sent packages in the post, though there was no doubt in my mind they came from Judith. They were romantic, not very grown-up gifts, the kind of things a teenage girl might send to the pop star of her dreams: teddy bears and oversized cards with poems written inside, sickly chocolates and books with apparently meaningful titles or subject matters, about the compatibility of certain signs of the zodiac, for instance. Also, my phone would ring and as soon as I'd answer it the line would go dead. (As an escort you can't afford not to take calls from 'number withheld' callers, because many clients block their phone numbers for privacy.) Her 24/7 calling became a severe irritant.

And then things got more crazy. I came home late one day and saw her waiting on the street corner outside my house staring up at my window. I dashed into the phone box near my house waiting for her to leave. It was a long wait. Nor was it the only time I saw her lingering outside my house. Another time, in the morning, I walked down to the lobby of my flat to pick up my mail and I distinctly smelt her perfume lingering in the air, but saw no sign of her. Either she had managed to get into the lobby or else I was imagining things and starting to go crazy.

In fact, that's almost what annoyed me most: not just her calls or the sightings I caught of her staring up at my window, but the times in between. I didn't feel threatened, not exactly, but the stress of wondering when I would next have to deal with her was like having a pneumatic drill going outside your bedroom window when you're trying to sleep. You hear the drilling and that's bad enough, but it's almost worse when it stops and you are waiting for the racket to start up again. The silence becomes as stressful as the noise. So it was with Judith. When it finally got too much I rang her up and told her this had to stop, that I couldn't see her again and never wanted her to call me for any reason, and that if she insisted on continuing I would change my phone number and then take more serious action (though of course as an escort I was hardly likely to call the police, but still there was no harm in letting her think I might).

That seemed to work. For a little while. Until she called me late one night and asked if she could come round for a session and because I was drunk and because I wanted to get paid (it must have been a slow couple of days), I broke my own rule about seeing her. Of course I was furious with myself as soon as I put the phone down. Now, I reasoned, the whole process would start up again and I was partly to blame for it. If you tell someone they have to cut off all contact with you, you can't then agree to have sex with them, not under any circumstances. My anger with myself and my annoyance with her was clear to her when she arrived (plus the drink had loosened my tongue). In many ways I think it actually served as a wake-up call to her and finally brought home the reality of what our 'relationship' consisted of.

'You don't want me here, do you, Andrew?' she said, hoping, I think, for reassurance and affection.

'You're a client,' I said. 'What do you expect me to say? But if you want to know the truth, not really.'

Our conversation went on along these lines until it was as if a light bulb went on in her head. 'Oh my God,' she said. 'You don't even like me. You're right. What am I doing here? I must be out of my mind.' When she said that I calmed down and did suggest gently that she perhaps seek some help, some kind of counselling, and she agreed with me. We didn't have sex that night and I never saw or heard from her again. For all her annoying phone calls and stalker-like behaviour I did feel sorry for her – it was obvious that there was something missing in her life and she – however misguidedly – thought I was the person who could provide whatever it was she lacked. But I think we both learnt lessons that night, and mine was if you lay down a rule, never *ever* break it.

When you first start escorting it's a steep learning curve. There's no gradual way in: you're either having sex for money or not. The most important lessons I learnt at the beginning were the obvious ones: as I've said before, to get the money before *anything* starts, and to be strict about time. The clock is on as soon as you open the door to a client or he or she opens it to you. You sit down and chat and have a drink together, of course: but guess what, that time must be paid for. *Everything* is on the clock. But there are also lessons that take longer to learn and only really sink in through experience. Learning about your boundaries is the obvious one, but you have to remember that there are always two people involved in escorting (or more!) and it takes time to begin to recognize or 'read' clients.

There are the collectors. Collectors are people you think you've shown a good time, but they never call again.

The first time as an escort you encounter a collector, you think, what have I done wrong? The answer is nothing. There are just folk who like seeing everyone once and only ever want a new escort. On the flip side there are those who come back a lot. Like those who go to the same cottage in St Ives every year, there are people who enjoy the familiarity of a regular escort. And then there are those who take regularity to an extreme. The ones who see you and feel that they've found 'the one'.

If I was immediately busy as an escort, that doesn't mean there weren't times when there was no work. Everybody in the sex industry, as in any business, observes lulls. Bank holidays, torrential rain, extreme heat, tube strikes, and elections: anything out of the ordinary tends to mean a slow day in the ebb and flow of business. My theory is that people use their *extra* time and money to see escorts – for some it's a need, but for most it's a bonus, so if there is anything that uses up their extra time instead, then you'll be shorter of business. Money plays a part too. December can be quite a lean month because people are spending so much money on other things, but right before Christmas things get ferociously busy because, I suppose, clients decide to treat themselves. August is the worst month because everyone is away. These lean times are always a worry. Even though you understand that there is a seasonal aspect to your job, you can't help but wonder whether this lean time may be the one when you need to take on another job, or tighten your belt a bit further. But equally there are boom times. The first week of April – with spring at last in the air – is always madly busy.

On an average day I might see two or three clients. Much of my business is last minute, which means I always have to be ready for it. So if my routine in Cambridge was to get up and go to the gym, I'd go to the gym having shaved, with my phone charged and my contact lenses in. I always carry everything with me – condoms, lube, diary, pen, Viagra, underwear – so I never need to go home if I get a call. Being a successful escort is as much about being organized as being gorgeous. You need to be up-to-date with your advertising, and websites if you have one or more. In this respect escorting is a job like any other kind of self-employment. It takes effort and time to get up to speed so that things run smoothly. Escorting is a business and a successful independent escort has to be the most organized of animals. Of course you can do it 'on the side', but if you want to make serious money, then you have to take it seriously.

One quick note: condoms are a given. Some clients might check that you use them, but most take it for granted that you do. It's very rare that you'd be asked not to wear a condom and if someone ever did they would be on a very no-go blacklist.

I've also got to be careful when it comes to alcohol and

drugs. While I feel no concern about not being cleaner than clean, the fact of the matter is that alcohol and drugs – particularly cocaine – impair my performance.

Women always take the full hour and more if they can get it to spill over. I am happy to kiss women and penetrative sex is nearly always involved. Sometimes it's hard to know when to stop. Of course if they come – or pretend to come – then it's easy, and in the main women who pay for an escort tend to be quite highly sexed, on top of which the thought of hiring an escort is a huge turn-on for most of them – that's why they do it. Often they are like a powder keg ready to go off, but that isn't always the case. Sometimes I just don't know what is going on inside them, sometimes they don't orgasm (or it's hard to tell) and sometimes I get tired. Sometimes, I have to say, I doubt my own ability – even male escorts suffer performance anxiety from time to time, though by now I've learnt enough strategies to cover up any feelings of insecurity I might have on the job. Whatever happens I hope I treat my clients with respect and thoughtfulness, in terms of what they want or what they are responding to.

The fact of the matter is that being an escort means that you often have to be economical with the truth – whether it's pretending that you really want to be with them when you'd rather be in bed with a good book or telling your client you find her attractive when she's really not your type – and that's part of the whole 'fantasy' experience. To be a good escort, you also have to be a good actor. But take acting too far, and dishonesty creeps in – a lot of escorts bend a few rules here and there.

For example, one regular client of mine always paid for a cab on top of my usual fare. But what I'd do was ride my bike over to her house and lock up my bike round the corner from her place. One evening we went through this whole drama of why I was a bit late. I explained it was because of the taxi and yes, wasn't it tedious when taxis deliberately took you a roundabout route and what rip-off merchants they could be, and when I'd finished, the client gave me the fare and then said, just as casually as you like: 'Ah. I was just wondering, because you've got your bike light clipped onto your back pocket. It's still flashing.' I put my hands up then. I was caught red-handed, what else could I do! But we turned it into a joke. It was funny. The session went better because of it. And I kept the money. It's the same thing if you can't get a hard-on straight away. Instead of getting embarrassed, I'm ready with stock statements like, 'It's a grower this one. Just encourage him because he's shy.' Then I smile and it normally does the trick.

Sometimes, women make out that really the whole paying thing hardly exists and that I am with them because I want to be. But even with my favourite female clients, it still comes down to a bottom line and that is that I am being paid. Still, I try as much as possible to take my time with my clients and make sure they are satisfied, and that means trying to get inside their sexuality, rather than thinking about my own. After all, women think about sex differently and are turned on differently from men. My old Sunday-school teacher (who was very forward thinking to be giving advice on sex) told us that women were like electric ovens and men like gas ovens. Women take time to heat up and cool down, whereas men have a simple on/off switch. I learnt a lot in Sunday school.

It's in the evening when business typically gets going, and nights vary. I often get calls at 2 a.m. It might be that I'll go to a London hotel for a long job or an overnight. I'm often called to the apartments of the very rich in places like South Kensington and Mayfair. There, I'm nodded through the doors by security guards and into private lifts to go up to private suites in enormous apartments. I've also been called to tiny cottages, filthy caravans and all manner of housing estates.

I got used to leaving hotels in the early hours, seeing the delivery vans arriving, the behind-the-scenes staff kicking into action – all the activity that goes on while most people are sound asleep. I like that, being privy to details most people never see, being the only person wandering down a street with my pocket full of money, hearing not the pigeons as you might expect but the unmistakable call of ducks and seagulls on their early-morning flight across town.

And the clients? The clients are always different and yet always the same. No one is special enough ever to be anything more than a client – that's the bottom line – though of course over the years I've made friends, had favourites, been more attentive and less. Some clients want what I call 'the boyfriend experience', where you are as attentive and flattering as they hope their boyfriend might be; others just want a quick fuck. I've worked harder for some than for others, being treated well and badly and all in all given as good as I've got. Let's just say, I don't think anyone would accuse me of being an angel. Sometimes things just don't work out from the get go. The most important defensive weapon you've got in escorting is your instinct. It's not always right, but you have to trust it and if you smell that something is wrong, then you leave. Straight away. *With the money.*

I've been called to a hotel room by a man and wife only to find that there are two men waiting for me instead. If that happens, you leave. If you have to justify taking the money anyway, you say: 'You've called me out, messed me about, how could you forget to tell me there would be a second male here?' And if you haven't got the money – if they won't give it to you – you leave without too much fuss. When things are not as they said they would be, what's next?

You also get funny situations in hotel rooms. I walked over to the Charing Cross Hotel near Whitehall once for a job with a businesswoman in town for the night. She was extremely cautious, opening the door to me with great care so that under no circumstance would she be spotted by her colleague who had the room next door. I entertained her for an hour and a half – the sex unexpectedly exciting, as we had to be as quiet as possible to ensure that the woman next door wouldn't know a thing. I left her room quietly so the colleague next door wouldn't hear the door opening and closing, and went down to the hotel lobby – the very place where Dr David Kelly, the UN weapons inspector in the Iraqi war, was soon to have one of his last cups of tea with the reporter Andrew Gilligan.

I checked my phone, as I always do, only to discover a message from another businesswoman in the very same hotel wanting to be entertained as soon as possible. She also asked that I arrive at her room very discreetly. That wouldn't be a problem, I told her when I called her back. Especially as I now knew exactly where her room was – right next to the door I had so recently and quietly exited! The woman told me that she and her colleague had seen my advert in a listings magazine and discussed it while having a bit of a laugh about what it would be like to call the number. Of course neither had any idea that both had actually followed the discussion one very crucial step further! I tried to imagine them over breakfast, hiding their sexed-up smiles from each other as they read their newspapers and ordered their eggs.

Mostly, I've had a lucky run. Until recently. I began escorting so cautiously that I haven't had many times when I wished I'd left a situation. I started, after all, when I was twenty-five, which is relatively late. While in one sense I was naïve, in another I was mature. I had been a church leader. So although I didn't know what on earth I was doing with the first police couple, there was another side to me that kicked in relatively quickly – and that side had already seen things that many people my age hadn't. I'd sat with people suffering long-term pain, facing the prospect of their children dying.

In fact, Nikki, the black woman I had my first duo with, was someone who wasn't so lucky. After our first time together, we started doing duos regularly, and often they would carry on after the client had left. I discovered that, despite what she had told me the first time we met, Nikki loved foreplay and loved me going down on her – in fact, she taught me a couple of tricks that I've used on some clients with great success. We weren't ever a couple, but we enjoyed being together, and I knew that she liked the fact that she was more experienced than me, that she could teach me things.

Then one day I tried calling her. Her mobile was out of service. I didn't really wonder too much about that – perhaps a client had become a bit too pushy and she changed her phone number; it happens. But then, after calling round to her place one day, I bumped into a friend of hers. Nikki had been deported, on the grounds that she had been trafficked. She had been sent back to Africa and a precarious life of poverty, a life where her choices were limited. She was now a statistic, a number in the government's fight against human trafficking even though she had come to England of her own free will knowing exactly what she would be doing. She now lives in a country where the average age of death is forty-seven.

I'd had several major epiphanies in my life, you might say, and acted on them. I understood a lot, which is why I became confident quickly and wasn't easily manipulated. Right from the beginning I didn't spend my money but saved it. I began from a very early stage to take my profession seriously, and I had an eye on getting out from the moment I got in.

CHAPTER 6

I've Got The Brains, You've Got The Looks, Let's Make Lots of Money

Of course this is the story of my life as an escort – and though it was fast taking up most of my time and I took it very seriously, it wasn't my whole life. I've never simply been an escort and nothing else. For years I was a student and almost as soon as I began escorting successfully, I started buying houses which I then let out and investing money in other places as well. My life felt full, even if I wasn't quite decided about my professional future. I had thought, while doing my MA, that I would go on to do a doctorate. It seemed a respectable thing to do, and because I was offered a funded place to do one – not an easy thing to get – I thought I should take it up. I'd escort and save up some money and then start studying seriously again. I could always do a little escorting on the side after all. But in April of 1999 I

94

made a firm decision about my life. I abandoned my plan and my place to do a PhD.

I thought, very consciously: I'm not going to do that. I'm not going to study and be an escort on the side. I am going to throw myself into escorting properly, come what may.

I'm not sure if I knew I was signing up for the secrecy and the stigma, the risk (and excitement) of living close to the underbelly of society, or if I just slipped into what I felt then, and still do now, wasn't such a big deal. I expect it was a combination of the two. I did think: I'm going to choose this work and this life for myself. It made too much sense financially for me to give it up and I liked the buzzing around of it all, as well as several of my regular clients such as Cheryl and Antiquity Woman.

If I was going to be a serious escort, I wanted to make serious money. I was choosing escorting in order to break the insane cycle of giving your best years to work. Instead I was determined to have my best years for myself. But to do what you want, you have to make yourself financially independent.

What did I think I would do with all my freedom? All my hours of liberty? What would define my life if I was free from wage-slavery? You needn't worry that I feared being bored or lost. If I was financially secure, I knew I could do whatever I wanted: travel the world, fall in love and get married, spend time with the children I hoped to have, put time into my relationships, work for a charity and give something back. In fact, by the time you're reading this, I can report that I've visited five continents and twenty-five countries, and I'm now either exploring my twenty-sixth, or in a room with a view courtesy of Her Majesty's Prison Service.

It's not all easy rewards. I had one client who was a senior politician, who'd been at the centre of things during the Thatcher/Reagan years, and whenever there was news of someone well known getting caught in a sex scandal (such as President Clinton undergoing an impeachment trial for lying about his 'sexual relations' with Monica Lewinsky, and Jeffrey Archer having to drop out of the London Mayoral race because it emerged that he'd lied in court about his alibi when in fact he had been paying Monica Coghlan for her sexual services), the client would shrug and say: 'There's no fool like an old fool' or 'All men are boys'. As if that explained everything, and in a way it did.

My God, I have behaved like an old fool myself at times. I may be full of worldly wise stories about the sex industry, but in certain situations I've behaved like a total novice. And I can be bloody lazy. The money was flowing in, and the work was easy. And I was just about to meet someone who would change my personal and my professional life.

Hannah and I met over a mattress. There was a garden wall between us, it's true, but still, it was all about a bed. I'd always had girlfriends – escorting certainly hasn't changed *that* – but no one ever serious enough for me to let in on my double life in the early years. I dated a Russian girl for a while who took me to Moscow for her best friend's wedding – paid for, by the way, not by the bride's father but her ex-sugar daddy. But even though I became privy to some of her dad's dealings, I didn't reveal anything to her about my own secret profession. Moscow in the nineties was like the Wild West: nothing was done without an under-the-table deal. My Russian girlfriend's dad told me that, during the Soviet years when Western goods were banned, he'd driven a Russian car into which he'd secretly had a giant German BMW engine installed. Why not just come out and say it: that you're a member of the mafia? But then some things are better left unsaid. We all have our secrets. I just didn't know how to let any girl-friend in on mine. That was until I met Hannah.

I fancied Hannah as soon as I saw her. I was furnishing a house I had just bought to let, and quite simply she was the student girl next door. She came over to say hello just as I was moving mattresses in. She was wearing a low-cut top and a push-up bra, and we started talking. Flirting, really. She said that my mattresses looked nice and new and that she'd got a rubbish landlord who'd left her with a horrible bed and a sagging mattress. 'Really?' I say. 'We can't have that. Tell you what: I'm going to an auction tomorrow where I can get good-quality beds. I'll get you one. In the long run it won't be any bother or cost.'

The next day, I arrive at her front door with a bed and mattress for her bedroom. Needless to say, in the context of this ridiculously obvious flirtation, after a few drinks we cut the long run short. As soon as that happened, I realized that this was not something casual. It's not that I fall in love immediately with Hannah – I don't – but my instinct told me that something significant was happening. How can I explain sleeping with Hannah? Well, imagine you're on a short break abroad. Because you're only spending a couple of days there, you can only be a tourist, you go and see the main attractions, visit a nightspot or two, but – however enjoyable – you're only skimming the surface of the place you're visiting, and you know that your time there will soon be over. That's what it's like having sex with a client. Fun, different, but ultimately superficial. With Hannah, it was like having a ticket to a foreign country with no idea about how long you'll be there. Because you don't know how long you're there for you get to know all the little quirks of the locality, the hidden places and secret dialects. Having sex with Hannah was at once profoundly physical and extremely emotional. I had been in love before, but Hannah was the first person to whom I lost my heart completely.

Hannah was nineteen when we met. I was twenty-five. I may have been older and with a few more life notches on my belt, but Hannah was unlike anyone I'd ever met. She was full of life, with a huge personality, and she had the can-dos about her. If she wanted to do something, she just did it, whether it was jumping out of a plane, swimming with dolphins or taking on a black run the first time she was ever on skis. She was fearless. She was also petite with a perfectly formed dancer's body – a beautiful pert bum – and short, dark hair, a pretty face and eyes that are completely alive. There was something about her that were so special, so fresh and exciting and different to any other girls that I met. And, perhaps, I saw something in her that I needed, something that I didn't even know, until I met Hannah, I was missing.

Hannah told me she was about to start her second year at nursing college. We discovered that we both went to the same gym. I recognized her cheeky grin; it was not unlike my own. And she had a way with her own instinct too. She knew as soon as we met that there was more to me than met the eye. Why else did I have two mobile phones – and this was back in the late nineties before owning a mobile became standard – if I wasn't up to something like drug-dealing? Plus, I let her use one of them all the time, even for long-distance calls, without any concern for my bills. But why would I care about calls made on a phone given to me by one of my more generous clients, a client who had significant stocks in very solid companies, who I called Sonia Blue-chip, a phone that was specially rigged up to generate no bill whatsoever.

A no-bill phone wasn't the only thing Sonia Blue-chip

gave me. She was a rich South African heiress and businesswoman who was always surrounded by an entourage
to do her bidding. Gifts were easy for her to give out, but
she still expected something in return: not merely a trophy
'boyfriend' or the boyfriend experience (that alone I might
have been able to do, and after all the money was excellent), but for me to show her subservience in public while
playing the dumb toy-boy – a role escorts often have to
play, in one way or another, and one I struggle with.

Sonia was a large, tall woman with a huge personality,
enormous asset portfolio and absolutely no sex appeal, not
for me, in any case. She was, despite her bravura and
bullying ways – or maybe because of them, profoundly
insecure. When she was in London, which is where she
was based, she lived in a suite at a famous hotel. As well as
looking big, she talked big too. Why was I worrying about
my degree? she said soon after we met. She could take care
of my financial future, she added, no problem. And
Madonna, she said, would be coming to one of her parties
– but then Sonia was always talking about all her celebrity
friends, only a few of whom I ever saw her with. She was
quite indiscreet about her famous friend, which meant
that the press were on full alert, waiting to see whatever
fabulous outfit Madonna might arrive in. Needless to say
she never did.

Sonia Blue-chip offered me lots of things. I once asked
her if I looked OK and she said: 'You can't improve on

perfection,' which made me feel good, I admit. Compliments do; flattery is hard for anyone to resist. But I did learn, after a couple of months of being at her bidding, that actually what I had and what she wanted was not for sale – namely my freedom and control over my life and my time. I turned down the 4x4 that arrived and was offered as a gift. I refused to move in with her. I stopped answering her every whim to go to this or that party.

But a curious (though I'm sure not uncommon) thing happened: the more withdrawn and detached I became, the more ridiculously possessive, manipulative and demanding Sonia became in response. She would do things like ring me up and find out what I was doing when we hadn't planned to be together. 'I'm in Cambridge, at the gym,' I might say, which would be true. But then I'd come out of the gym and find her driver waiting there for me with a Rolls to take me to London. I should have known better and ended the 'relationship' sooner, but that's the nature of being manipulated: sometimes it's hard to see through the fog of confusion and bullying, especially if you are greedy.

And greed, I'm afraid, was my Achilles heel. Money was what made me get up in the morning. And that's why I didn't stop agreeing to see Sonia Blue-chip, no matter how difficult she made my life.

Sonia Blue-chip suffered terrible attacks of jealousy and couldn't bear for me to have my own independence. I found it incredible that someone so forthright was also so insecure, but that's the way it was. The driver would tell me I was needed urgently and I'd get in the car only to arrive at Sonia's hotel suite or offices and discover that nothing was going on. I'm not interested in these sorts of games and power struggles. Sonia liked it that I wouldn't be talked down to – that was part of my attraction – but at the same time she couldn't handle the fact that I refused to be controlled by her. And her temper could get the better of her.

After a few months, I'd had enough. I'd earned a fortune, sure, but at what price? I realized that no matter what money was on offer, I had to retain and keep sacred my own independence. How did I break it off with someone so controlling, paranoid and threatening?

Sonia flew off the handle one day, screaming and shouting about 'our relationship', and I told her I found her behaviour unacceptable. I reminded her I was an escort, that I had boundaries and that this was not in my remit as a professional. I told her I had had enough, that I was in charge of my own time and that I was leaving. Sonia couldn't believe I would do it, that this wasn't mere histrionics and drama, but that's what you have to do: walk away. And I did. I had to leave via the back way, however. Sonia called security, and I had to leave via the fire exits in order to avoid a fight I'd definitely have lost.

I didn't get off that easily, however. When she realized I

really had gone I received a phone call informing me that her gold credit card had been stolen and that I was under suspicion. Plus Sonia somehow managed to have a couple of cheques, which she'd written to me and I had paid into my account, bounce. So I was left feeling worried about being accused of something I hadn't done and being out of pocket. It was a nightmare – I had lost cash, and that was hard enough, but what was worse was that in some way I become powerless over parts of my life: as if the police were going to come knocking on my door at any moment, and the uncomfortable feeling that came from knowing just how easy it had been for Sonia Blue-chip to take money from my bank account. It was a highly emotional time for me, and for a long time I had a horrible feeling in my stomach from the moment I woke up until I went to bed – I knew Sonia's reputation, and I had seen at first hand her treatment of her staff – and I mentally prepared myself for her to avenge herself on me. My worries never came to pass – perhaps she thought that stopping the cheques was enough. But I had learnt something from my time with Sonia, and that was that I was determined to remain in control. I also decided not to accept cheques for payment. From now on, it was cash only. That was, until the next time.

It's also true that there was another factor in making me come to my senses with Sonia. Hannah. I may not have been ready to commit to her or tell her about my life, but I did, I realized quickly, want to be free rather than a kept man so that I could see her. Meanwhile she, of course, thought I was a drug dealer. I didn't like her theory, but I didn't tell her the truth. I don't think drug dealing was her ideal career choice for a boyfriend, either, but that doesn't stop her being attracted to me, and in fact if anything it turned her on – she liked a bit of naughtiness. When I met Hannah she was young and relatively inexperienced and though she had never had a puff on a cigarette, didn't eat meat and had never been into drugs or drink in any big way, she was ready and eager to suck the marrow out of life.

At the beginning, I tried to keep things fairly casual and at arm's length – if you don't tell someone you love them and you resist going steady, which is what we did for eighteen long months, then you can still keep a few things under wraps. She never asked me about my professional life, because she intuitively took the 'don't ask, don't try to find out and don't tell' route in terms of information. After all, if you ask questions, you may not like the answers.

Still, Hannah was not averse to playing the system herself. Soon after we met, she discovered that one of her friends' sisters worked bang opposite the venue for that year's Brit Awards. That was like an invitation to the party as far as Hannah was concerned. She and her friend borrowed a high-resolution digital camera with a long-range lens, were let into the building by her friend's sister, then took a photograph of the security guard standing outside the venue, focusing specifically on his entrance pass. They put the image through the computer and somehow produced a near-perfect replica down to the pass's fake silver identity square. It's amazing what you can do if you're a dab hand with Photoshop.

She's the sort of girl who would go to the Brit Awards and get into the innermost VIP sanctums where both champagne and pop stars are flowing liberally. You have to remember that Hannah was a nineteen-year-old trainee nurse living in Cambridge and brought up in the provinces. She didn't have media connections or experience, and yet there she was, where she wanted to be that night, sitting between Liam Gallagher and Mel Gibson, having a laugh, without ever taking any of it too seriously. I may not have any interest in pop music, but I loved that Hannah didn't just love it, she made something happen out of it. She bent the rules. She was naughty. I liked that.

I realized, as weeks and months went by, that I liked Hannah. A lot. Being an escort may not be as hard as you think it is – but the secrecy thing? The secrecy thing is harder than you can ever imagine. Forget the effect living a double life has on your psyche for a moment – that's one thing – but it's the million other potential pitfalls that mean you have to live your life constantly not being able to show the real you.

One time I met Hannah's family and we went to see

Graham Norton live. In his routine of the time, he used to flick through the classified adverts at the back of magazines and then phone escorts for a comedy chat live on the show. You can imagine my horror when I realized that he was reading out the advert next to my own, to the merriment of the audience. And, I realized, he may be about to dial my number. I couldn't turn off my phone because then it would go to voicemail and Hannah and her family would hear and recognize my voice requesting any potential clients to leave *all* their details. Thank goodness he strung out the jokes and the dialling long enough for me to frantically phone my own voicemail and turn off my message. On this occasion, luck was with me, but I did realize, once again, that I couldn't be too careful. That's why it was weird that, eighteen months after meeting her, I was sloppy enough for Hannah to discover what I really did.

I sent an email to the escort agency Suited and Booted from Hannah's computer. I was interested to see if Suited and Booted had any Cambridge work for me, but of course when they replied to me that really they only dealt with London and New York, the email came to Hannah's Outlook Express account. Why was I stupid enough to send an email from Hannah's account? To this day, I'm not entirely sure, but perhaps, when all was said and done, I wanted her to know, and it was easier for her to 'discover' the truth than for me to tell her outright. As soon as she read it she put two and two together. Well, that wouldn't have been hard, but what was a surprise was her reaction. 'I've got something I want to talk to you about,' she said to me, and as soon as she said that my stomach dropped to the floor. I knew she knew.

'It's about your job,' she continued. 'I think I know what you do for a living and it's not drugs. But frankly, unless you are hiding a whole secret stock pile of suits, you must be the worst-dressed escort I can think of!' Just like that, the secret I had been keeping since 1998 collapsed. Suddenly someone knew. Not only someone, but my girlfriend, and not just a girlfriend but the woman I was in the middle of seriously falling for. My stomach was in knots, and I sat on her bed, prepared for Hannah's anger, or her shock or her recriminations. But none of that happened. Unbelievably, Hannah *wasn't* shocked. On the contrary, she wanted to hear about it. She wanted to know every detail.

So I told her. Everything. It was make or break time. I figured that if this relationship was going to work, if it had any possibility of getting serious – which, more and more I was hoping it would – I had to tell her the whole truth. Either Hannah understood and accepted what I did, or she didn't, which meant she wasn't the right person for me.

We stayed up all night talking. I told her about how I would do duos with other escorts, and how occasionally those duos would carry on, after the client had left. I told her about going to students' rooms, about my liaisons with rich and charming women, about the clients who weren't so rich and charming.

Hannah asked questions, but mostly she just listened to what I had to say. The first thing she wanted to know was whether I was safe – which when I told her that I was, she accepted at once. She knew from her own experience that I am very conscientious when it comes to that sort of thing. And she wanted to know whether I had ever been emotionally involved with any client – I could tell her truthfully that I never had.

We had been sitting on the floor in a room lit only by candlelight for hours. An empty bottle of wine sat between us. Dawn was breaking and light was beginning to slant in through the curtains. My throat felt rough and sore from talking. There was nothing more to say; I had told Hannah everything and at any time she could just get up, walk out the door and leave our relationship behind her. There was always that possibility. But at the same time I was feeling hopeful. She hadn't left... yet.

'So,' Hannah said eventually, 'you're saying that you've almost got too much going on with your property business and your escort work...'

'Both could be really successful,' I admitted. I thought I could see where she was going with this. 'But it's still early days and I can't give up escort work and just work as a property developer. And I enjoy what I do so I don't want to leave the business and become a suit—'

'That's not what I mean,' Hannah interrupted. 'I can see that your escort work brings in a lot of cash.' I was about to say something but Hannah held up her head to stop me. 'I have to say,' she continued, 'it's not for me. But what about this...'

There was a twinkle in Hannah's eye as she set out what she wanted to do. I would continue escorting – she was fine with that, in fact, she liked the fact that her boyfriend was so wanted and desired by other women that they were prepared to pay for him – while she would take over running the property business. What did I think of that?

'I think,' I said, reaching over, grabbing her ankle and pulling her towards me, 'that that's a very good idea indeed.'

She laughed, and playfully tried to push me off her, but I grabbed her wrists and pinned them up above her head, kissing her until her giggles subsided and she started responding to me with the same passion I felt for her.

Hannah may not have wanted to be an escort, but in many ways we were very alike. We wanted easy cash and at the time escorting and property were two easy ways to get it. Hannah was already disillusioned by her chosen career. She was a trainee nurse in a hospital and she'd had that feeling you get when you pass your exams and the fireworks don't go off. It's like, oh, so this is what I'm working so hard for? To be paid like a monkey and treated like a dog. To work hard all day doing something that is not going to give me enough money to buy a house.

Meanwhile she saw me, who seemed perfectly happy and not damaged or weird or a low-life, who was buying houses like they are going out of fashion. She qualified that summer, immediately started nursing on minimum hours only, and started taking on more and more of my property business, while I concentrated on bringing more money in by escorting.

Hannah was a rare find, in that she could separate sex from love, at least at this stage in our relationship. She knew that when I had sex with other women, in duos, that it was just that – sex – and nothing like what we had together. When she first found out about my life, she was remarkably sanguine about it, which I think had something to do with her high self-esteem and confidence. She didn't worry about the clients I was having sex with because she knew she got the real me, not the persona I put on for everyone else.

Also, if it wasn't for my escort work, she wouldn't have been involved in the property business, she wouldn't have had the designer bags and shoes or the long days spent pampering herself at a spa. I also think for Hannah there was a vicarious risk in being involved with an escort, without being an escort herself.

And Hannah worked hard. I gave her a percentage of what I earned in property as payment for taking on the business side of things and not long after we started working together she bought her first buy-to-let. It turned out that she was an astute negotiator. You didn't sleep on a dodgy mattress if you rented a room from Hannah, but on the other hand try being late with your rent. Soon after that, she and I bought a house together. Everything seemed to be working out for us.

I have to admit something here, though. In the early stages of my relationship with Hannah, I had become close to a girl who I had also met in the course of renting out property. Her name was Jodie, she was a tenant of mine and gorgeous – long blonde hair; cute, perky little bottom; golden skin – a natural beauty. And intelligent too – she was studying Politics at university.

Although she always paid her rent on time Jodie was clearly struggling with money. I would go round to her place when called to fix furniture and other odd jobs, and she would make me a cup of tea and joke about how, if she was careful, she'd be able to save up for that Pot Noodle at the end of the week. I liked her, she was fun and bubbly and was the kind of person who tried to put a positive spin on things, despite the powers that be having decided she wasn't eligible for financial support.

One evening I was booked to do a duo with an escort I hadn't worked with before. By now I usually sorted out any duo work myself, preferring to work with women I knew and trusted. But this evening was slightly different. The guy was a regular – he liked to masturbate while watching a couple having sex, sometimes he'd join in, sometimes he wouldn't. He paid very well for the privilege and also tipped well.

I arrived at the hotel at the appointed time and knocked on the door of the room. It opened, and standing there, a smile frozen on her face when she saw me, was Jodie. I think I was as shocked as she was although I tried not to let it show – I knew that money was tight, but I never would have thought that she would have ever considered escort work. Wasn't Politics her thing?!

I gave her a reassuring wink and walked into the room. The client was pouring us both a glass of champagne. I could see that Jodie was nervous, so I held out my hand. 'Richard,' I said, introducing myself by one of my aliases.

'Jodie,' she said, shaking my hand.

Jodie had just broken one of the first rules you learn as an escort: never use your real name. Along with the nervous way she was acting this made me think that escorting was new to her.

'So,' I said, 'why don't we get started?'

The client concurred, and poured himself a large glass of champagne. 'I'll sit down over here,' he said. 'Why don't you take her clothes off?'

Jodie smiled up at me. She was clearly still nervous but she wasn't going to back out now. I unzipped her dress and it fell in a puddle on the floor. Reaching behind her I unclasped her bra. Jodie stood there, in just her panties.

She really was stunning. I wondered how long it would take for the client in the corner to stop watching us fucking and take over.

I took her over to the bed and started to caress her breasts, my hands reaching round to pull her panties off that beautiful bum. Her nipples grew hard under my touch, and she looked up at me, her expression changing from one of nervousness to one of excitement. I knew that the client liked to see a lot of foreplay, so I ran a line of kisses down Jodie's stomach until I reached her pussy. She was wet and soon was writhing under my tongue. It wasn't long before she came, pulling my head up as she did. She reached down and started to stroke my hard-on.

'Why don't you bend her over the bed,' the client said. He was stroking himself, obviously turned on by Jodie's very genuine climax. I put on a condom and turned Jodie round so that her fantastic bum was towards me. I slipped inside her and she immediately started moaning.

Just then a mobile started ringing. I knew it wasn't mine – I'm always careful to keep it on silent when I'm with a client. Jodie looked back at me. 'Shit,' said the client as he looked at the screen. 'Shit. I have to take this.'

The client, his hard-on subsiding, stalked into the bathroom. I pulled out of Jodie and sat on the edge of the bed. Jodie turned round and sat beside me. 'This is weird,' she said.

'Yeah,' I said, 'Just a bit.'

Just then the client came out of the bathroom. He explained, as he quickly pulled on his clothes, that a deal he had been working on and thought was in the bag now looked as if it was going to fall through and he had to get it back on track. He had to leave. We, however, were welcome to stay as long as we liked – the room was paid for, after all. He left, still doing up his tie.

'Well,' I said, moving to the champagne bucket. 'We certainly shouldn't let this go to waste.' I poured her a glass of bubbly before topping up my own.

'Thank you,' she said, giggling. 'You know, this was my first time – well, with another escort. I've done a couple of jobs before, and I've got to say, I'm pleased my first duo was with someone I knew.'

'Cheers,' I said, clinking her glass with mine. 'Glad to be of service.'

We spent the rest of the night in the suite, with Jodie asking me loads of questions about being an escort. I have to admit that I told her everything I could to put her off. Wasn't she concerned about the dangers? Didn't she worry about what she could be letting herself in for? What about her college career? And then there is the safety issue, though an escort can go years without getting into trouble. In ten years of escorting, I've rarely been in a fight, but then I'm a talker, not a fighter. A friend of mine and fellow escort, Elizabeth, is always in trouble. When she rings me to tell me that a client of hers has gone wild because his money is missing, she always adds: 'But of course I didn't take it, it's just that he's gone mad because he thinks I have.' And there is no point trying to get the truth out of her. But it's funny how often the same person finds themselves in a fight or in trouble, and yet it's never their fault. I should listen to myself! I told Jodie all my fears and still she was adamant. This was the only way she could see of getting money while making sure her studies didn't suffer. She was sick of worrying about where she was going to find the cash to pay off her mounting student debts, as well as day-to-day expenses such as rent or money for food. Instead of trying to put her off, she suggested, why didn't I tell her how things worked. And, she pointed out, I can't be doing too badly for myself, not if I was able to also own property and be her landlord having been a student myself only a couple of years earlier.

Basically, she was not going to take no for an answer from me, and so I figured that if she was so determined to give escorting a go, then at least I could help her start up properly. It's a big deal to begin escorting and not something anyone should go into lightly. After all, I was sitting on all this hard-earned knowledge, so why shouldn't Jodie have the benefit of it? So here I was, lecturing the university student – 101: Introduction to the Life of a Sex Worker.

Later that night I got even more of a surprise. We were pretty drunk by then, and as I poured yet another glass of champagne (we had ordered room service, charging the champagne to the room – we knew that the client's credit card would be charged and that he wouldn't question it), Jodie sat up and sung, 'Majesty, worship His Majesty...'

I replied without thinking, 'Unto Jesus be all glory, honour and praise...'

We both stopped laughing and stared at each other. 'No,' said Jodie. 'That's just too weird. Are you... were you...?'

'I was going to be a missionary, yes,' I admitted. 'Until I saw the error of my ways.'

Jodie laughed delightedly. 'And I was a youth group leader, looking after the kids at Spring Harvest...'

'You didn't,' I said. I knew exactly what she was talking about. Spring Harvest is an annual Christian gathering with an attendance of 80,000 people. 'I did too!' We realized we had been at the same venue in the same year.

'Crazy,' she said, shaking her head. 'To think we must have met at one of those events.'

'Crazy,' I repeated. And then, thinking, I said, 'Listen. You really shouldn't use your real name. I think it's time for a re-christening.' I held the glass above her. 'In the name of the Father, the Son, and the Holy Spirit, I baptize you... Eden!' I said, pouring some champagne over her head.

'Eden!' she giggled. 'I love it!' and we kissed.

It turned out that Jodie was a natural escort and we worked many times together. We became really good friends. I felt protective towards her, and was always willing to give her advice, and to call her for anything that needed someone who brought a great deal of charm and sincerity to the work. One of our favourite jobs was with well-known film correspondent. Working together for someone like him was a pleasure.

Alistair was not interested in having sex with escorts. He was a voyeur. He liked to film people having sex and he was happy to pay for it. Mostly I've got zero interest in doing porn. You get a few hundred quid for it, it takes all day and you don't know where the film is going to end up. It's only really worth it if you make it big, and those are precarious odds.

Alistair was different though. Being paid by him to have sex with women on film, which he would then watch, worked on many levels, not least because he wasn't at all overbearing, never overstepped the mark and always behaved like the perfect English gentleman he was (he lived alone but still used a butter knife, for instance). It was also a handy way for me to meet and connect with other female escorts, which is useful for future jobs. He had a portfolio of photographs he'd show me and I'd be able to pick a girl for the next session. Or else, he'd tell me to bring someone of my own choice if I wanted to, and so naturally enough in time I brought Jodie – Eden.

Alistair loved to watch male and female escorts undress, lie down and naturally masturbate or have sex, and he was so unassuming and gentlemanly that when Jodie and I did sessions for him, we had sex for real. Fuck it, we thought, let's just do our thing rather than putting on a show. Rather than having rampant, energetic sex, with us athletically throwing ourselves around the room, or trying to get into the right position so that our bums didn't look too big on camera, we were tender with each other, took our time when undressing and gazed into each other's eyes. Alistair was so polite, his clothes were always on, he never touched us or himself while he was filming and he much preferred us to do what came naturally to us. He could have hired a porn movie if he liked the fake stuff, and even making his own films he mostly saw women faking their climaxes, which is fair enough, but it rocked his world when Jodie came for real. He was also consistent. He liked reality across the board, and so didn't mind if you didn't get the hardest erection in the world on occasions. When you're doing a long, protracted photo shoot, you don't want the blushed look of Viagra face in the photos – one of the hazards of the job.

One day, after we finished filming, Alistair told us that that was to be the last time he would use us. He had skin cancer which had metastasised into his lungs and the doctors said that he wouldn't have long to live. After a long fight with his illness, Alistair died peacefully in his sleep. It was terribly sad, of course, and Jodie and I toasted his memory over a bottle of wine. I remember his obituary in

The Times (Alistair was a journalist and a correspondent for a well-known broadsheet newspaper) when he died. 'He never married,' the writer said, which is an obituary euphemism, of course, for being gay.

But Alistair wasn't simply a 'confirmed bachelor'. He was interested in women. He may have been more interested in men, but women weren't just in the margins for him. 'He never married' is not the whole story – I wanted to write that to the newspapers after the obituaries came out. Alistair was incredibly discreet and had left written instructions with his lawyer that his room full of archived sex tapes and, later DVDs, some dating back to the sixties, be destroyed on his death, but I also think he would have enjoyed having his sexuality celebrated. I don't mean he ever wanted to be outed, and Alistair isn't his real name. I've got no desire to expose anyone, but I honestly believe he'd be tickled if he knew I was writing about him now, and about the fact that he was far from asexual, that he had a full, lively and satisfying erotic life and one I'm so glad to have been a part of.

Often the most unlikely people do. People you think lead lonely lives in terms of their sexual experiences have often found ways to satisfy themselves. Sometimes those ways may seem bizarre, but as long as they aren't hurting anybody, why does it matter? Where's the victim? And often, especially for more unusual desires, an escort is the easiest and safest way for some people to explore what turns them on. An escort I knew, and a long-standing friend, had one client, for instance, who wanted to be hurt. He wasn't after an S&M experience so much – there are many professional doms (or dominatrices) for the submissives out there – as just straightforward pain.

I've been asked to wear everything you can imagine. It's not uncommon for someone to say, could you wear yesterday's unwashed pants, or maybe they'll ask me not to wash my socks. A lot of people have shoe fetishes, but it's not just the old cliché of licking stilettos that turns some people on. One woman loves loafers. I didn't even know what loafers were until she asked me to wear some. It didn't occur to me that she'd be obsessed with suede slip-on Hush Puppies. She would buy them for me and when I went to see her I would bring two small rucksacks of shoes with me, then walk around in my underpants and shoes, all different kinds of shoes, until I built up to the precious suede loafer and she couldn't take any more. She would kiss them, stroke them and worship them.

I go along with the theory that some people get stuck in the moment of their sexual awakening. Think how many people are into spanking (old Etonians often ask for it) or dressing up as schoolgirls (you have to be eighteen to enter my websites by the way). But I'm just an escort, and it's just a theory.

CHAPTER 7

Newton's Third Law Of Motion

Newton's third law of motion is that every action has an equal and opposite reaction. When Hannah and I moved in together in the summer of 2001 it was great fun. Of course it was a relief to be able to share our life – every aspect of our lives – with each other. And yes, we were awash with money. We were busy buying up houses and running them as a profitable side business, but it wasn't all larks, high jinks and oodles of cash. Life is never that easy and escorting gives you many things but a complication-free life is not on its list of promises.

Soon after Hannah and I moved in together we cele-brated the second anniversary of our first date, on 10 September 2001. We splashed out on a night in London, going out for a meal and staying in a hotel, somewhere nice and convenient in the centre of town but nothing super fancy. We may have been making a lot of money but we were also spending it wisely, not on flashy hotels but on our housing business, which for us equalled security, future and freedom. It's absolutely true that money doesn't buy happiness. But what is equally true is that it does increase one's choices.

Still, we'd had a big night out and on the train home fairly early the next afternoon we both turned our phones off in respect to the occasion of our anniversary. Only obviously mine wasn't turned off – it never was – but was switched to silent. That meant I was still receiving messages and just after lunch I began to see a flurry of missed calls from a fairly regular, pretty normal bread-and-butter client I called Bristol Susan. Moments later the same Susan sent me a text message saying 'Twin Towers in NYC on fire'. At the same time as I read the text I began to notice the atmosphere on the train changing – as other people began to field calls and receive the news – news that was getting more and more tragic as the minutes ticked past.

I was, like everyone, profoundly shocked and saddened by what had happened. I couldn't quite believe what I was hearing, or that life in Cambridge would carry on as normal. That I still had to sit on a train that a driver continued to drive, that when I got off I still had to go and return a deposit to some Chinese students who had recently moved out of one of my houses, still had to pay bills and do chores and return Bristol Susan's calls. It amazed me that I, her escort, would be important enough to her that she called me as soon as she heard the news. All over the world people were calling their nearest and dearest to share their shock and grief and Bristol Susan had called me? (Some time later she told me that I was the only thing that had kept her alive during a period of severe depression, which reminded me of the very human side of the sex business and how the job I do can fill all kinds of holes in people's lives, rather than just the obvious ones – if you'll forgive that little flippancy.)

Hannah and I held each other until we reached Cambridge. I still had to run errands, yes, life was continuing, but nevertheless nothing felt the same. Nothing was the same. And mostly we cancelled our plans for the day so we could watch the news uninterrupted, like so many people around the world. But I had to return the deposit to the students as I had promised.

To this day, I have an odd reminder of 9/11 – not that anyone ever needs reminding of such an unforgettable tragedy. But one of my closest friends, Catherine, whom I've known for years, had been in New York when it happened. She was on her way to the Twin Towers when the towers were attacked. The only reason she wasn't actually having breakfast at the famous windows on the World bar and restaurant, admiring the view of New York from the top floor of the highest skyscraper in the city, was because she and her friends, hungover from a night on the tiles, were late starting their day. She was close enough, though, to witness the horrors first hand. And to take pictures, though she couldn't bear to have them developed until a year after the event. But she did do one odd thing, as people sometimes do in times of stress. She bought a little globe with tiny models of the Twin Towers inside – one of those souvenirs that you shake to make it snow on your chosen cityscape – and she gave it to me with its receipt showing the time – an hour after the Towers fell – and the date – 9/11/2001.

But however much you think your world has fallen in or changed, there is one thing you can be certain of: people will still be having sex. It was also a time when people reminded themselves of what their priorities in life were and what was important to them. Intimacy became more important to many people, and though for most people that meant spending more time with their families and loved ones, some people – people unable to do that for one reason or another – sought out new people for physical contact, an escort for example. This was how I came to meet the Croupier.

The Croupier was in her late thirties and she had a fantastic body, which she showed off in amazing outfits she made herself – PVC catsuits and corsets and things like that. She told me when I first saw her that the recent happenings in the world had made her want to explore her sexuality more – hence hiring me, a young escort.

The problem was that although she seemed totally at ease with paying for sex, she behaved when we were together as if she wanted more: she treated me like a boyfriend. Of course this is fine – in many ways that's my job: to arrive at your house and, for an hour or however long you've hired me for, become your lover (or whatever it is you want me to be! As I discovered, not everyone is looking for affection or wants to pretend – some people just want straight, uncomplicated sex). It's just that that has to be done within a certain time-frame and with certain boundaries.

The Croupier didn't stalk me or behave badly in any way, it's just that she wanted more than I could give her. Often this manifested itself in the effort she made when she booked me for an appointment. Not only would she open a bottle of wine, but she'd have made little dips and eats. That wasn't all. She made me clothes, not unlike the ones she wore herself when I saw her. That was her turn-on – anything tight, small and preferably made of leather or PVC, and so she'd present me with tiny leather Speedos or a skintight wrestling-type outfit.

Again, fine, it's just that she'd then ask if I'd been thinking of her since last seeing her. At the beginning I'd just laugh it off, but she got quite insistent with her queries. It gets to the point where there is a difference between pretending one thing within the confines of an hour and a specific set-up, and actually lying about what the reality of a situation is, and that reality is: I'm an escort and you're a client and no I don't wear your PVC briefs off hours. Also, I found the sex demanding – not in the physical way that Cheryl insisted on, but in a way that made me uncomfortable. She wanted, for instance, me to stroke and caress her for what felt like hours, while whispering loving things into her ear. The thing was that that's what I do with Hannah, and in my mind there is no overlap between the two. You have to have some things that you keep for your partner, just like Nikki kept foreplay for something that was just between her and the guys she slept with for fun. It was starting to get too emotional on the Croupier's part and I just didn't want to go there with a client. Plus I found the outfits a nightmare of discomfort and so after a while, whenever the Croupier called, I found myself fully booked up and unavailable for wine, dips, PVC, sex and sweet nothings.

Plus, I was busier than before. I wanted to spend more time with Hannah and my friends after 9/11 rather than working so hard and making money. I'm glad I did this, because it turned out that one of my friends, Steven, was to die in Iraq, during a war that I myself, though an uncomfortable protestor, marched against, along with two million other people, in March 2003.

I met Steven when he came to look round a house I was selling. Five minutes after he'd seen it and clearly got rid of the estate agent I was using for the sale, I received a cold call from him. 'You want to sell the house,' he said, 'and I want to buy it. So let's cut the estate agent out and deal with each other directly.' He couldn't have been more straightforward. 'And while we're at it,' he added, 'I want you to tell me the best way to let it.'

I knew immediately he was a right naughty boy. Not that that bothered me. And he let it be quickly known that he knew I was up to something more than buying and selling houses too. I suppose it was a bit obvious when he dropped round one day only to find me in my dressing gown having a cup of tea with a female escort I'd just done an in-house duo with for a couple who wanted to spice up their sex life by having a bit of a foursome. Not that Steven was shocked. Far from it. He wasted no time at all in asking the escort if she was finished working for the afternoon. 'Depends what you're offering,' she said flirtatiously to him. Steven was a good-looking, well-dressed alpha male. Most female escorts would be quite happy if all their clients were like him. 'Whatever you're worth,' he said back to her. They didn't talk for long, and I shrugged my shoulders and smiled when she asked me if my room was going to remain free for the next hour or so.

'It was like a porn movie,' Steven told me later about their encounter. 'Coming into your house and finding a gorgeous hooker drinking tea in her underwear, as if she was waiting for me. I even enjoyed paying her.' I'm pretty sure Steven became a regular client of hers, at least for a while. It couldn't last. In 2003, Steven called me. 'I'm going away,' he said.

'Going where?' I asked him. 'For how long?'

'I'm just going,' he said. 'Tonight. I don't know how long I'll be gone for. I'll call when I get back.' Then he asked me to keep an eye on his properties and collect any rent he was owed, which of course I was happy to do. And that was it. I didn't hear from him for seven months, not a word. Nor did he respond to emails. I collected his rent for him and made sure the house was in good nick, but I had no idea where to pay in the money he was owed, so I kept it safe for him.

Eventually I heard from him, or rather he returned to Cambridge and started buying houses, paying for them with exorbitant amounts of cash. Tax-free cash, at that. And don't imagine he paid any council tax on his properties either. It transpired that Steven had been in Afghanistan on and off for the last few years, earning huge amounts doing incredibly dangerous work as 'a private security guard'. In 2004 he went to Iraq and did the same thing. A few months later, in early 2005, Steven was killed on an airport road in Baghdad.

Although we knew that Steven's situation in Iraq could only ever be precarious at best, neither Hannah nor I were prepared for the news. Somehow, we had thought that Steven, with all his vitality and lust for life, was invincible, that somehow bullets would just pass him by. I felt anger at him that he had taken such risk for money.

Steven knew what he was doing and the risks involved. He still chose to do what he did. Likewise I knew that what I was doing came with its own risks. I'm not necessarily talking about violence or the possibility of bodily harm, though of course that can happen if you are an escort. No. A much more likely scenario is blackmail. It comes with the territory, yes, but that doesn't make it any less upsetting. Blackmail intends to scare and violate its victim, and though my blackmailers didn't succeed in making me give in to their demands, neither could I escape the psychological effect being blackmailed had on me.

The first time I was blackmailed was via email. It lasted a year and it was horrible. The first email, sent to my advertised email address (and therefore not to my real account or under my own real name), was simple enough. It asked me what services I offered, what college I studied at (I advertised myself as a student) and if I had a West Country connection, which was odd because of course I was brought up in Cornwall, where my family still live, but that was hardly something I screamed and shouted about. 'Hi,' I emailed back, all bright and breezy. 'No real West Country connections. Just a dead grandmother from years ago. I'm from Chichester. Do call if you'd like to know more.'

The next email I received from this apparent stranger used my real name and asked me if indeed I was X from

Cornwall as he or she was from the same area. Now, that's the sort of email you don't want to get as an escort. That's the sort of email guaranteed to freak an escort out. Especially one whose parents are born-again Christians from a small town in Cornwall and know *nothing* about his secret life. Could it be someone from the Church? Was this a former client who somehow knew my parents? Had she recognized me from one of my websites? True, I used photographs of other people on my sites to ward off any potential discovery – models who looked similar enough to me not to disappoint clients – but had this person twigged somehow?

The emails continued, asking me about my brother (who was named) and my home life. I was upset, but, quite frankly, I was also pissed off. How dare this person – whoever she was – blackmail me? What gave her the right? Did she have any idea of the hurt she could cause? Not just to me, but to my parents, to my brother, none of whom had ever gone out to hurt anyone in their lives? And, like with Sonia Blue-chip, I felt powerless against the onslaught. This just made me angrier. What I was most furious about was the fact that there was nothing I could do about it.

In the main I tried to ignore my email pursuer in the hope that the less fuel I gave her – the less I appeared to react – the quicker she might tire of provoking me. But then I'd get an email like this: 'X. Why are you ignoring me? I'm making a few local enquiries. I believe I'm known to your parents. You must be careful about how you advertise. You must be careful. There is so much at stake from someone from a religious background.' That last phrase reassured me. It's the moment I thought that actually these emails are probably coming from a client, rather than a stranger who knows my family in some way. A Christian would use the expression 'from a Church background' rather than 'from a religious background'.

That made me think that my emailing bully might be Judith the Stalker or even the Croupier. Both had gleaned quite a lot of personal information about me because they were so insistent on conversation. Both were possessive and minded that I 'saw' other clients. Both felt that in some way I should be their loyal boyfriend. Desire and longing and fantasy and dreams of escape and matters of the heart have nothing to do with rational thought or your day-to-day actual existence. And matters of the heart, every so often, can prompt people into taking extreme action. Like blackmail.

Pretty soon the emails turned nastier and more threatening. I tried ignoring them, then tried responding asking to meet up (I just wanted to get to the bottom of it all). I pulled all my advertising to try and pre-empt further damage. Nothing seemed to work. 'What would your parents and brother think about the disgusting things you do?' the emails would read. 'The local newspaper would be very interested in your line of work, don't you think?' When I pulled my ads they wrote: 'Glad to see you haven't been advertising for a couple of months. Does this mean that you have given up your sordid business?' But when I rerun the ads (I still have a business to run after all), using different photos and a blurred-out face that isn't even me and a new phone number, he or she gets back on to me again. 'See you are back in *Time Out*. Don't you think your parents deserve better? Won't you stop? You must be earning a packet. Share it about?' And then: 'I have copies of your ads. I wonder if I should send your parents a few goodies. For Christmas?'

The emails went on for a year. Christmas at home was a nightmare with me rushing down to inspect the post every morning before anyone else could get to it. I soon stopped responding at all to any of the threats. I offered to meet the person to 'discuss things', but they lost their nerve and refused. Eventually the emails petered out and then stopped. But it was thoroughly unpleasant and upsetting. I dreaded opening my email account every day, and the worry that someone might upset my family so terribly was awful. It also meant that I shut down part of myself with even regular clients.

Blackmail, as I have said, is something that happens to any good, long-running escort. It is a way for the client to take back the power they perceive the escort has over him or her. Why else would they want to bring such turmoil into someone else's life by bullying them and threatening to expose them? It's their way of saying I'm reclaiming power over you because I perceive that you are more powerful than me in this situation, where I have to hand over money for what I want, and I'm going to punish you for that. Blackmail, like many other forms of violence and abuse, is often about power and control.

Not many clients feel like this. Most are easy to please and perfectly satisfied with the relationship between themselves and an escort. But there are the exceptions: those who are experiencing distress in their sex life, which can then take over much of the rest of their life. Escorts can be used as vessels to channel some of those feelings. And because an escort is vulnerable and can't go to the police, there is not much he or she can do about it except either sit it out or take matters into his or her own hands.

Jodie (the Politics student/tenant I had taken under my wing) and I managed to do this to one of her blackmailers, though it didn't make the experience any less brutal for Jodie to go through. She was blackmailed more than once too.

The first time it happened, someone – clearly a client of hers – put leaflets through all her neighbours' doors telling them they lived next door to a prostitute. Jodie had always been extremely discreet, and none of her neighbours could have had any inkling about her secret profession until then. I know several escorts who have undergone the same treatment. It's horrible. One of her neighbours came over to her house and showed her the leaflet. 'Do you know who Eden is?' the neighbour asked her. What can you say? You just say, 'Eden? Who is Eden?' And then, when the door is closed and the neighbour has gone to bang on the next house, you decide to move out. That's how I learnt about Jodie's trouble – she called me up to say she needed to find a new place to live and could I help her. Luckily I could, and was happy to do so And of course when one of her neighbours contacted me to complain there was a prostitute living in my property, I was indignant in Jodie's defence, saying 'I know her to be a woman of great integrity devoted to her studies and from a good family' and purporting to be shocked and stunned 'by these lies about one of my best tenants'. I know other female escorts who have lost six months' rent because they have been chased out of their flats so quickly.

Leaflets were one thing though. Jodie was blackmailed much more seriously a second time when she appeared on a then hugely popular light entertainment TV programme. Only in the lag between appearing in her first and second programmes, she foolishly drank too much champagne one evening and told one of her clients about her TV adventure. He attempted to blackmail her. He threatened, very seriously it seemed, to go to the tabloid press and reveal her true occupation unless she slept with him for free. Jodie called me, in tears, and still feeling protective of her, I sprang into action. There was no way that I was going to let anyone, let alone someone I felt such a brotherly love for, go through the turmoil that I went through when I was blackmailed. I wanted to do everything I could to protect her from that. Jodie told me she had a regular client who was a senior police officer and another who had served for many years in the police force and had now retired. I suggested that we should go together to talk to them, to see what they could do about this guy.

The officer was happy to help. Nobody likes to hear about a woman being threatened and bullied, and this man had chosen his profession based on his desire to protect people. He also knew the danger his whole team were in if the story broke and too many details were revealed. He looked up Jodie's blackmailer on the police database and discovered he had a previous conviction for GBH on women. He also found out where he lived, how he owned his house, what car he drove, where he worked. Not quite what he ate for breakfast, but almost. And then he and his colleagues gave him a taste of his own medicine. They went to his workplace to ask questions about him. They pulled over his car because his wing mirror wasn't right. They went round to his house to check up on something else. They just were on him, basically. And when he started feeling properly harassed and began to complain, they told him to fuck off, not talk, or things would get worse. Meanwhile someone vandalized one of his classic cars by pouring battery oil mixed with sugar over it, which gives it a sticky corrosive viscosity.

They didn't waste any time and so the man was stopped in his tracks. But for Jodie, things had been spoiled. She didn't enjoy any of the media stuff because she was still so fraught with worry. Even though we reassured her that her blackmailer had been stopped, she couldn't help worrying that on Sunday morning, the night after she appeared on the programme, there would be headlines in the red tops exposing her as a prostitute.

It was a brutal time for Jodie. She, who had always been bubbly and vivacious, seeing everything in the best possible light, lost that innocence. Something in her began to change. She became cynical, a little hard-bitten. What had at first been a lot of fun for her was suddenly hard work and draining. Sure, Jodie had gone into the business with her eyes open, but that didn't mean she was ready for all the pitfalls, or to learn the hard lesson that every action has an equal but opposite reaction.

CHAPTER 8

The Body Politik

Hannah and I broke up. What can one say about a relationship that fails? It just didn't work, or we didn't work hard enough at it. Of course, we were both devastated, but neither of us could see any way that we could stay together. I'm not sure how much my work as an escort contributed to our break-up. It's not really something that I can speculate on. The fact is we were fighting more and more and, to be honest, being together just wasn't that much fun any more. We both have strong characters and in retrospect neither of us was willing to compromise enough. We preferred to go our separate ways rather than stay together and tough it out.

Or rather I went and Hannah stayed. I wondered about moving to New York and decided to place a few ads on websites and in publications over there to see if I could attract any business. This was in the era of cheap travel. It was also the advent of Internet sites like Craigslist, which made escort work abroad easier and more plentiful. Sex sells whereever you are and the novelty of being some- where just for a week is a great pull – the key is to use a small number of great photographs on your site. (Many escorts are reluctant to put photos of themselves online, and the solution is to use a photograph of someone else whose looks are similar and to blur their face. Most clients never guess and don't care anyway, as long as you are then truthful about who you are and what you look like.)

Similarly review sites (written by clients about escorts and how good or bad their service is) are frequently used as forms of advertising. It's easy to place a positive review written in the third person locating yourself wherever it is you want to go to and saying how fantastic it is that this town or city has such a great new escort.

This is what I did when I first went to New York. I rented a small apartment in the East Village, and the night after arriving I was booked in for my first job on the Upper East Side, for a couple I had seen several times in London who also had a smart apartment in New York. My female client and her husband were not retired coppers or estate agents or a middle-aged bored and unfulfilled couple. They were aristocrats living a transat- lantic high life. Not that they told me much about themselves. But you can tell certain things from the amount of security people have. The private lift. The doorman who doesn't raise an eyebrow even though I'm arriving at 2 a.m. The fact that they did all their 'business' with me in an anonymous wing of the apartment they clearly had little other use for, thus indicating the huge amount of space that must have been available.

They were both immaculately turned out, in their forties I would say, though it's always hard to tell when people are so well groomed. She had ultra-straight blonde hair; he incredibly groomed. He wore Gucci loafers, pressed jeans, a striped shirt and silk socks. She was in a short dress that draped over her and should have been tarty but somehow was just sexy. She looked too rich and expensive and glossy to be tarty. Like a racehorse. When I described the dress to a friend later she said it must have been silk-jersey and was probably designed by Tom Ford at Gucci. How do women know these things?

The problem is, the fantasy is always better than the reality, threesomes are never quite as sexy as people hope they will be, or at least in my experience, and sometimes I think they should come with a government health warning on the side. Or maybe they work for two of the three, but inevitably someone ends up feeling somewhat left out. Feelings of jealousy are very quick to surface. In this case the atmosphere was rocky right from the start. First of all, I could tell that they were both drunk and high. They were smoking marijuana and offered me some as soon as I arrived. I don't smoke dope. It's not good for me. For one thing, I can't maintain an erection after even just a couple of puffs of the stuff, and secondly it can freak me out. I can't smoke it, period. Plus I wonder about this couple and others who do drugs before hiring me: if they are so into having a bit of kinky sex with a hired stranger, why do they have to get out of their heads to do it? And is she really so into it anyway? Or is the real client the husband?

Ostensibly, it's the woman who was my primary client. She was the one who called me, booked me and, presumably, chose me. She's the one who always paid me as soon as I arrived. And yet I got the distinct impression that she was doing it *for* her husband – to excite him, rather than as something that was a genuine turn-on for her. It felt like she was acting the part of the volcanic sex fiend underneath her perfect dress and ironed-straight hair. The threesome felt forced. Mainly it was her and me with him watching and not much joining in. I could understand him not wanting to touch me, but not wanting to touch her? She was gorgeous. She was his *wife*. Was this all about putting on a show for him?

We began by taking off our clothes. At least, the wife and I took off our clothes: he took off his shirt and that was it. The wife had a perfect, gym-toned body and had shaved her pubic hair into a perfect landing strip. I touched her full, beautiful breasts – which I guessed were false but I couldn't tell, and she arched her neck, which I kissed. I pulled her down on to the bed, lifted her legs on to my shoulders and started to lick her pussy. She was responding, but I could tell that her attention was less on me, and more on her husband, who was observing the proceedings with a look of cool detachment that made me start to feel contempt for him.

Trust me, I think I know when's the time to move away and let the couple get on with things by themselves, if that's what begins to happen, but in this case it didn't. He just carried on smoking joints while I had sex with his beautiful wife. Did she enjoy it? I don't know. She seemed to, but no more than if she were using a vibrator. It was a very detached sort of enjoyment – sometimes she moved so that I was entering her from behind and I wondered if this was so she didn't have to look at me (or was the smell of marijuana making me paranoid?) Such detachment of course is fair enough considering I'm an escort, someone paid simply to come through the door, take off my clothes and get down to business. But usually, if you've been hired by a woman, then you are part of a fantasy. Usually it's the client who wants the escort, and the escort who wants to hide.

I don't kid myself that my clients necessarily have any emotional attachment to me, but mostly they are invested in what they are doing, what they've paid for and, on the whole, have looked forward to. But this glamorous, perfectly bred woman? No, there was none of that with her. My impression was that this was a woman whose marriage was stymied. They may have looked great on paper, this couple, you may even have seen photographs of them at parties and events and envied them their lifestyle, but they didn't seem to be having much fun to me. Their penthouse may have been enormous, but there wasn't much love in evidence. Frankly, I felt sorry for them and was glad to get out when the session came to an end.

I love New York and, like many people who visit the city, feel that I could happily live there. Clearly there would be enough work around. But it didn't translate economically for me. At the time the pound was so strong and the dollar so weak. I had to face up to the fact that in London I could get more cash per orgasm than anywhere else in the world. Plus, if I worked in America without a work visa, I would be working and earning money illegally and therefore not able to lay down serious roots even if I wanted to.

If I knew I wanted to return to England after my stay in New York, I was equally sure I didn't want to return to Cambridge. After living there for so many years I was bored. I had a portfolio of properties there and a full client pool, but I no longer felt challenged. I also didn't want to run into Hannah at the gym or in the supermarket or at one of our favourite haunts. I didn't harbour bitter feelings towards her but I did feel some regret that we hadn't worked it out. In many ways we suited each other so perfectly. I knew my love for her hadn't vanished, but we hadn't been able to live together without rowing all the time. I wanted to move swiftly on from those feelings of frustration. I decided it was high time I settled in London.

The first thing I had to do was to find a flat, and it turned out that luck was on my side. I was looking at the properties in an estate agent's window near Liverpool Street one morning when I overheard a heated argument between a female estate agent and her male boss that was taking place on the pavement outside the office. I didn't catch the details of what the fracas was about but I did hear the boss call the woman a bitch.

I interrupted his name calling and told him where to go. I was in my bodybuilding phase at this time, going to the gym still very much part of my daily routine, and so I wasn't someone you might take on. The estate agent skulked off and I made friends with the woman and told her I was looking for a London flat. I told her as much as I could without revealing what I'd actually be doing inside the flat and promised her a couple of grand if she could find me something that would suit me.

Two K was a bargain for me. It was much cheaper than travelling up and down to London and losing vital escorting hours looking round endless flats. It was much easier to leave it all in the hands of this woman, whom I instinctively trusted to find me the right place to start my London life. She did too. A small studio flat in Pimlico, close to Victoria bus station which offers easy access out of

London to the south-west to see my family in Cornwall. It was also central enough for clients and yet perfectly anonymous. Many politicians have their London pied-à-terre in Pimlico, while keeping their main residence and their family lives in their constituency. The area has the feel of people coming and going and not quite settling. Put it this way: you don't see too many baby buggies there, and it's unlikely you'd run into someone you know doing a spot of shopping, in the way that you would if you lived in Notting Hill, say, or Primrose Hill. Plus, crucially, I could afford it. Mind you, it was pretty small. No, it was tiny, with little ventilation and not much charm. But it was mine and, if I could make a success of things in London, I knew it wouldn't be for ever.

In Cambridge I had developed a reputation, I was one of the few males escorts, but London is a much bigger city, more anonymous, less easy to break into. I was going to be a small fish in a big pond, and I was nervous to know if it would work out in London. Now, I feel like a Londoner, but back then I didn't feel entirely confident I'd be able to make it. I had friends from my childhood and university who lived in the City, plus some of my clients were London-based. Cheryl, living in Essex, was closer to London than Cambridge, and my work with Antiquity Woman would continue, only at her London base rather than her large Cambridge pad. She had a new escort anyway, a much better-looking black guy called Anthony whom she was mad about, and so our 'relationship' had developed more into a friendship. Anthony, I hear tell, is very good at his job – certainly he has a no-nonsense approach to advertising. His ads run with the caption, 'For Fuck's Sake Get Fucked!' It clearly works a treat for him as I believe he has a string of famous clients – the bastard. Why does he get all the interesting jobs? Still, it was Anthony who introduced me to someone who became important to my professional London life.

Jonny Bedlam is a pimp. I use that word deliberately for its negative connotations, because actually it's a word we rarely use in the sex industry. 'Agency owner' is the usual term, and one that rightly doesn't have the same sinister baggage, but with Bedlam there is no other way to put it than 'pimp' because that is what he has become. He doesn't actually wear the stereotypical pimp's hat and a leather coat, but he's not far from it. Jonny Bedlam isn't Jonny's given name, but it is his proper name now because he changed it by deed poll. It shows his commitment to leading a life outside society's norms, and being heavily involved in the more chaotic side of making money. He's a confessed natural-born sociopath – and, if it gets him what he wants, he will tell you anything you want to hear. Bedlam, when I first met him, in 2002, was twenty-three. He'd already been working in the sex industry for eight years. You name it, he's done it. He's earned and lost a fortune, several times over, basically by being involved in anything that isn't above board, from pimping to producing porn videos, from selling Viagra, illegal drugs and DVDs, to scams and facilitating the crossing of borders for people joining his agencies. He runs both male and female escort sites, sites for duos and sites for himself. Normally I'd say that the caricatures of people in the sex industry painted by the press and reinforced by government agencies aren't a true picture, but in Jonny's case they are spot on. And the fact is, Jonny Bedlam can exploit people as much as he wants. He's a reason to decriminalize the industry if I ever saw one. If the industry was properly regulated then people like Jonny Bedlam couldn't operate.

Whatever you want, Jonny Bedlam can get it for you. I'm not saying anything we haven't said to each other in private, because the fact is we don't really like or trust each other. I'm happy with that arrangement. He's extremely talented, one of those people who organizes the world around himself, and he has surrounded himself with people who adore him and will do anything for him. He's gay, though happily sleeps with women for money, and both men and women go for him like moths to a flame. He is black, handsome and charismatic, but more than that, he seems to inspire a kind of hero worship. People seemed to get addicted to him. Maybe that's also to do with the kind of people he surrounds himself with – yes-men – or yes-boyz – basically. But Bedlam also has good points beyond his great charisma. He's an escort's escort. A prostitute's pimp. He's like a captain who has come up through the ranks and instinctively understands what's going on in any situation. When I first met him, introduced by Anthony, he agreed to take me on and give me bookings in return for a commission, which is standard for any agent. But most insist that you are with them exclusively, whereas Bedlam doesn't care. He's smart enough not to try to micro-manage his escorts too much, and in turn they reward him with a certain kind of loyalty. He cares about what all those who run agencies care about, which is that your phone is on and you are ready to go, and that if he gives you a job you show up, collect the money and give him his third without cutting him out or trying to poach clients. Whatever else goes on, as far as he's concerned, is between you and the client and if the *client* doesn't like it the client is wrong.

I can understand it, but I think it's short-sighted that more agents aren't as supportive of their escorts, or for that matter why escorts aren't more appreciative of their agents. Some of them, particularly, it seems, among women, actually look down on their escorts, which I find pretty rich.

Half the work, *and it's a lot of work*, is doing the advertising, running websites, answering the calls, getting the job, dealing with money, screening the clients. If an agent can do that for you, they deserve their fee. My view is if you don't like it, don't use one, it's as simple as that. And if you do use them, always, always pay them. Don't try and 'go private' with a client they've provided. They'll find out in the end and as a result will punish you by not giving you work. Pay them. And pay them on time. It's annoying having to meet your agent on a Friday morning, say, to give them a cut of your earnings after working all night on a Thursday, but that's the way it goes. If you play by the rules and treat your agency right, they are more likely to do the same in return. The online agency Suited and Booted, which closed not long after one of their escorts was found to be the partner of Lord Brown, the head of BP, may have been picky about which escorts they would take on, but once you were with them, what they cared about was reliability and trustworthiness. I showed up to my appointments on time, always made sure I paid them promptly and correctly, and as a result the work flowed in. It helps, of course, if the person who runs the phones and makes the bookings has a soft spot for you, and I've mostly been lucky in this respect and always been given a lot of work.

For a time, Jonny Bedlam was a brilliant agency organizer. I made more money from him than anyone else and his so-called agency was just him in his bedroom working from an old computer, something none of his customers would ever have been aware of. But his life seemed to spiral downwards as time went on. He seemed to relish going from agency organizer to pimp. Sometimes I feel like he's become stuck in a moment – why does my instinct say that if he doesn't give up this life he'll be dead in four years? I remember how rich and successful he seemed when I first met him, only I don't know what he's done with all his earnings. When I last encountered him he was living in a scuzzy squat in Soho. Where did the money go? Perhaps he was robbed or fleeced or perhaps he just wasted it. All I know is that after a while I didn't want to work with him any longer.

I learnt a lot about the sex industry when I moved to London. It had been easy to ignore some of the seedier sides of the business living in Cambridge, but in London you aren't allowed such insulation. For example, the sex business in London is multi-tiered in a much more formalized way than anywhere else in the country. Of course, prostitution goes on all over the place, but nowhere is it quite so organized, hierarchical and abundant as in the area covered by the tourist pop-up map.

The Home Office estimates that eighty thousand people work in the sex industry on a hands-on way in the UK, a tiny fraction of whom work on the street. Street walking is the clichéd view of what prostitution is, but it doesn't come close to the way most sex workers live and work. Of course it does go on and every so often it comes to the forefront due to some awful tragedy, such as what happened in Ipswich in 2007 when five street-working women were brutally murdered by a single client.

Prostitution is seen as a dangerous profession – it's

certainly more risky than the average office job – but on the whole, contrary to received opinion, sex work is usually quite safe. Of course, the Ipswich murders hit us hard as a community. We may not have known the women personally, but we did know women like them. The problem is that it often feels as if there's not much that you can do. To combat that feeling of powerlessness I became involved in organizing, amongst other things, the End Violence Against Sex Workers Day, which is held every year on 17 December.

There are, of course, different types of sex worker. One level up from street walking is to work in 'walk-ups'. These pretty much only exist in London's Soho. On certain streets a 'model' has a notice outside a door of the anonymous-looking sex establishment and if you are looking for sex you literally walk up from the street. That flats are sometimes disgusting. I feel sorry for the women working in them. They are run by Madams who make a fair whack every day and you'd think the least they could do is paint the place or put a new carpet down.

Next is working in a 'flat'. Every town in the UK has flats. It's usually just a suburban house with two working girlz in it. A client can only visit a flat by first telephoning. How do they get the right number? Either from an ad in the back of a local paper or, if in London, from those horrible cards you see plastered all over every phone box in central London.

I'm not against people wanting to work but the practice of telephone-carding with semi-naked pictures in a public place? Why do they think that's OK? I wouldn't want my mum or my nephews or nieces seeing that when they come to London for the day. The argument from the sex industry is often that 'they are just earning a living' or that 'it's a place where the very poor can advertise' but this is basically bollocks, because the truth is that it is only a small number of people, who run multiple flats, who advertise in this way, using multiple names and numbers and getting an advertising space without the consent of the general public.

Of course the police could easily catch the carding boyz employed by the madams and stop the practice, but they don't because there is a truce between the police and the people who run flats and walk-ups. The thing is, you can't stop a natural market and the police know that. If you start to do a clear-out of one area, it will simply move on to another, and while it's moving it will be a lot more visible and unsettled. The better way, in my opinion, is to regulate and tax the sex industry. Using both the carrot (regulation and protection) and stick (taxation) approach would force the industry to smarten up its act and look after its workers. Furthermore, if the industry were to be decriminalized, this wouldn't mean that there suddenly would be new laws. Rape is illegal, as is theft and assault. What would happen with decriminalization is that when a sex worker is robbed, assaulted or raped then she or he would be more likely to go to the police, and there would be more likelihood of her assailant being convicted, meaning that the streets would be safer for both sex worker and civilian alike. That's why the British Home Secretary's proposed changes to the law on trafficking and control for gain in 2009 are such a bad idea as they will drive the vulnerable away from access to help.

A brothel is a flat or house with more than two girls working in it. Again, they exist all over the country, though are less common than flats. The brothel usually has the veneer of respectability or 'good health' about it, often promoting itself as a massage parlour.

An agency, by contrast, only deals with out-calls, and sends escorts to the client rather than the other way round. An independent escort is someone, like me for most of my working life, who cuts out the middleman or only uses an agent as a back-up for extra jobs. In order to be able to do that you have to be willing to run your own business, set up your own websites and run your own advertising. It's hard work but if you can cut it then financially it's the top of the tree. That is unless you cross over into sugar daddy or mummy territory, or even into mistress/marriage status. But that's a different story. And, of course, there are many other ways that people sell sex.

As I became more aware about the complicated workings of the sex industry, as well as some of the myths about it, I decided I wanted to get more involved in having control over my and my co-workers' professional lives. I joined the union. The International Union of Sex Workers, or the IUSW, is a rather disparate group of lefty people working in and around the sex industry. It became a more formalized organization when in 2002 it joined the GMB, or Britain's third largest 675,000-member-strong general union. I couldn't be less left-wing in my politics but I'm so proud of the GMB for accepting the sex workers as part of their organization because the sex industry is made up of people without labour representation, and joining the union gives those without a voice a platform from which to speak. There was no way I felt I could abstain from getting involved. I emailed the branch secretary of the IUSW and started regularly going to union meetings – which turned out to be about as sexy as a mid-week early morning prayer meeting.

It was at a union meeting that I first met Innocence. Innocence is like an escort that Hollywood might dream up, only she's real and determined to make that clear. She's twenty-two, blonde, slim and American. She comes from a family of politicians, and she's very bright, very beautiful and knows how to use both those things. She's a high-class escort who runs her own websites, is in full control of her own career and earns a great deal of money on her own terms – at least that's what she says. What's her speciality? The most important thing: earning money. I love working with her.

She is also the most active person in the union. I almost fell in love with her, but God she's annoying. She wants *everything*. And because she doesn't have to work very much, she dedicated most of her time to being politically active, and not just in terms of sex. She's protested at Heathrow, and broken out asylum seekers from detention centres. Give Innocence a cause she believes in and she's up for it. I admire that. I just wish she didn't talk quite so much shit or was at least willing to listen to my shit too. The discussions at the lefty union meetings go on for hours. She has what I call the quickening, which is when you feel your blood racing and your heart rate increasing as cash is put into your hands – to keep. I recognize it in her because I feel it myself. And like most beautiful people, Innocence likes to be flattered. She likes to be told how sexy and wonderful and gorgeous she is (which she is), but at times I'm not sure whether I want to marry her or strangle her, this Marxist revolutionary in a Prada dress and La Perla underwear.

Mind you, at least she has actual experience as a sex worker, because most people working in charities and NGOs don't. They are academics or lefty activists who have done their PhDs about sex work, but actual real-life experience? No.

It's hard to unionize a group of individuals who are self-employed and don't have any natural meeting place, unlike say taxi drivers who go to the same cafés, use the same garages and become familiar with each other. Sex work is a long way from being able to appoint a shop steward on the factory floor; it's footloose, flighty, youthful and tax-free.

Still, despite my reservations, I'm a huge supporter of the union. I try never to miss a meeting. But I also think the sex industry politicos behave like a group of dysfunctional children in the way they argue among themselves about theoretical points. Such an uncompromising approach reminds me of a café next to my house which specializes in all-day breakfasts. The first time I went in there I asked for baked beans on toast and a couple of rashers of bacon.

'Not possible,' the woman behind the counter said.

'But you sell baked beans,' I said. 'And I can see that you do bacon and eggs. So what's the problem?'

'Bacon and eggs. Not bacon and baked beans.'

'But I don't want eggs with my bacon, so can't you just substitute the beans for the eggs and we'll all be happy,' I said.

'No,' she said. 'We don't do that.'

'But I can order eggs and bacon only without the eggs and a side order of baked beans with toast?'

She looked at me as if I was being unreasonable. 'We don't do beans on toast with bacon.'

That's what sex-work politics occasionally feels like, and the laughter of those who don't really care about what happens to the vulnerable will be our reward if we quarrel in this way. Innocence and I are at least agreed on this, and on the fact that the word 'trafficking' is being used unfairly by those who have a moral objection to the sex industry and so deliberately muddle the figures about it. (You can read more about this important but complex issue in Dr Belinda Brooks-Gordon's excellent book: *The Price Of Sex*.)

Innocence and I became friends despite what she sees as my insensitivity and stubbornness. After all, I'm no wilting flower either and we recognize much of ourselves in each other. We also agree that working together might be fun, and if doing a duo leads to a little crossover from work into pleasure, we won't be complaining.

CHAPTER 9

The Blind Leading The Blind

O ne of the lessons you need to learn as an escort is how best to store your cash. You can't just keep it stashed about the house. It's not working for you there, and worse it's not safe. Once I moved to London and started to get to know characters like Bedlam I realized I couldn't use my flat as my piggy bank because pretty soon someone else would catch on and help themselves too.

My rule became never to keep money in the house and to strategically leak that rule to people. After all, the person most likely to steal from you is someone close to you. That's probably going to be another escort or an adjunct to the escorting world. I once came close to being robbed when a female escort 'dropped round' unannounced one morning after we'd done a lucrative duo together. I wondered why she was taking so long to bring in the tea she had insisted on making. I found her rifling through my kitchen drawers, and it wasn't teabags she was searching for. Where was the cash? In the washing machine with a load of wet clothes.

On the subject of washing machines: *if* you are going to keep money in your house, here is a tip. Washing machines and many electrical devices have unusually shaped screw heads that you can't open up with a standard screwdriver. Of course, if someone's intent on robbing you, who absolutely knows you have a stash of money hidden away, they'll take your whole house apart, but if it's someone who thinks he or she is in for a let's-see-if-it's-here, then they are unlikely to start unscrewing casings on your washing machine, particularly if the job requires a specialist screwdriver.

Personally, I didn't go to so much trouble. I did a job once in a swanky Mayfair Hotel with what you might call a 'tease' of escorts and one spoilt New York banker. This was a really fun job. The guy wasn't really into me, but what he did like was loads of escorts, all at the same time, all at once. But nothing ruins the party like sex workers waiting around with nothing to do, so to keep the party going, he hired me. I knocked on the door of the room, and when it was opened by a stunning woman with long, dark, wavy hair, I was greeted by at least three other girls, all in various states of undress and in the midst of them was the banker, grinning away like a cat who got the cream. I dived straight in – it was a smorgasbord of food and sex. There was loads of champagne, of course, and masses of caviar and I sampled the delights of each of the women, while they caressed and stroked my body. It got to the point where I couldn't tell who was touching, or who I was touching, and we all ended up together, rolling about on the giant bed, a twist of legs and arms and bodies, covered in food and wine and sex.

When we were done and our fists full of money in the morning, they all told me they were off to Selfridges as soon as it opened to stash their cash. Selfridges? I asked. Yep, they said. They all had safety deposit boxes in the store in a section downstairs near the electrical department. I couldn't miss it, they said. I just had to head for the pricy pizzeria down there and the cash boxes would be nearby.

It's amazingly simple to get a safety deposit box at Selfridges. You just phone up. You don't need ID, it works by recognizing your signature each time you visit, and it costs, or it used to cost back then, £50 a year. Going to my safety deposit box and dropping in bundles of rolled-up £50 notes quickly becomes part of my bi-weekly ritual, as integral to my routine as shaving, putting in my contact lenses, checking my phone and going to the gym.

Cash isn't the best way of investing money though, is it? To me, property in those years took that prize, which is why for me there is ultimately no point in not declaring my earnings, because to borrow against money, after all, you have to officially have it. But not everyone is in the position to buy a house or start a business. Don't make the mistake of thinking anything happens automatically, or that being an escort equals an immediate roof over your head and a lucrative portfolio. Like anything, you have to work hard to make money being an escort, and you have to have some nous to make your money work for you. But yes, it beats, at least for me, clocking into an office, and it's what I call making money the easy/hard way. But even if you make a lot of money, and many women, in particular, do, a house may not suit you. You may not be paying taxes or have official status in this country or want to set down permanent roots. And yet, if you are Brazilian or Russian, say, and working hard as an escort, how are you going to get large amounts of cash back into your country and through customs if you can't mailgram?

It's a little-known fact that many Russians buy stamps. Philately first came to my attention when I was working as a language teacher. I did some overtime around then working with Russian foreign students, showing them round historic sites in London and making sure they all got back on the bus and didn't get stranded at the Tower of London. I'm not saying they were mafia kids – what do I know? – but all I can tell you was that out of eighteen kids in the group, two of them had fathers who had been assassinated back in Moscow. One of the fathers who was still alive had given strict instructions to his daughter that while she was in London she should visit a particular stamp shop on the Strand. When the father rang me I was immediately intrigued. She was to be allowed to be separated from the main group activity to go to buy some stamps?

Well of course stamps, like certain autographs, aren't just curios, but when bought wisely represent portable wealth. A single small stamp can easily be worth ten thousand pounds and its value doesn't change if you sell it in London, New York, Moscow or anywhere else. That's true of many things, of course, but the beauty of a stamp is that you can carry it through customs (unlike gold bars or wodges of cash or diamonds) without anyone ever being the wiser if they are discovered. And just in case all that wasn't incentive enough, their value has risen disproportionately to property, which, let's face it, is not exactly a portable wealth-storage system. If you are a Russian or South American escort and you have lost faith in your banking system then buying a stamp as a way of investing your wealth, never mind solving the problem of getting it back into your homeland, is a pretty attractive option. In the meantime, though, I decided to stick to cash.

I've got a friend who has a senior position in the police and often has important visitors to stay when they visit London. It was at a time when two American students were staying at my flat – I had since moved from the small flat in Pimlico into a much bigger one near Westminster tube – as they spent a year studying at King's College. Thinking I was free for a morning I told the girls there was no need for them to give me any privacy in the flat, only of course that's when the unexpected jobs always come up. This one was two lesbians in their thirties.

Why would two lesbians want to hire an escort for an hour? One of them, who had more experience with men, had decided to give her younger lover the experience of having sex with a man as a birthday present, and that man was me. Her girlfriend had never been with a man before and was curious to see what it was like, the older lesbian explained to me nervously on the phone when making the appointment, and so she wanted to give her this chance in a safe, controlled environment, perhaps joining in or taking over, depending on how things went. I guessed that there was an element of control in the older woman's gift – perhaps she was worried that if her girlfriend didn't see what sex with a man was like soon, she would look for it on her own, and this was her way of controlling the situation. Truth is often stranger than fiction in the sex business, and this request wasn't really that odd, not in the scheme of things. Anyway, she asked, was I up for it and could it be done now, this morning, at 11.30 a.m., before both lost their courage? I said I was and that it could. I then texted my friend in the police force, whose keys I have and who lives near me, to ask if

I could borrow her flat for a couple of hours while she was at work.

After all, her flat is empty all day, and even though she had given me the keys for emergencies only (if she lost her set for instance), what harm, I reasoned, could it be if I let myself in and used her flat with a couple of lesbians for an hour or two? When I didn't hear back from her I conveniently assumed that it was OK. I rang the women back and arranged a time to meet the two of them there at my friend's rather grand house. When they arrived they looked uncannily alike, both pretty and both wearing hers and hers Scandinavian-styled glasses.

We got straight down to business. The slightly more experienced woman sat on a chair in my friend's spare room and watched us while the less experienced woman, who was absolutely lovely, asked me to teach her how to give a blow job. It all felt a bit weird, the sort of thing that would be fine if done a little tipsy and in semi-darkness at night. At 11.30 a.m. in the cold light of a February day, it was hard for me not to feel somewhat self-conscious. It's also unusual to use your cock as a teaching device in such a matter-of-fact way, necessary in this case because the woman was insecure about her lack of experience. You have to keep it hard when what you are doing is treating it fairly clinically and, I have to be honest, my pupil was not a natural in the blow-job-giving department – who is when they start? And why should she be? She probably delivers magnificent cunnilingus but it must be a bit daunting being presented with your first erect cock, especially when your partner is fully clothed and watching you! It takes practice to get good at anything, oral sex included.

The other problem with the lovely lesbian was that not only was she completely inexperienced when it came to a penis but she had taken her glasses off and was clearly very far-sighted. I don't think she could really see what she was doing and that wasn't helping her nerves. 'Would you like to put your glasses on,' I said as kindly as possible, because I didn't want her to lose even more confidence in an already awkward situation. Plus, of course, she had been missing out on looking at both mine and her own body, which is all part of a sexual experience (and it doesn't matter what size or shape you are for this to be exciting). She actually laughed when I said this and some of the tension in the room began to dissipate.

We took a bit of a break and the more experienced woman told me they were both health advisors and so in theory nothing about the body shocked them, but that they still had to take their courage into their hands for this birthday celebration. I told them I wasn't surprised and that I'd have felt the same way in their position. And even experienced escorts get nerve attacks! I offered to help her give me a hand job and duly came for appearances' sake. But as we were talking and about to start again on our session, and as I was trying to think sexy thoughts in order to get a new erection, I suddenly noticed in the corner of my friend's spare bedroom a police uniform draped over a chair. I knew this meant only one thing: that a senior officer was staying in my friend's spare bedroom, the very room I had helped myself to and where I was being paid by two lesbians for a sex session.

My next thought was: the police officer could come back at any moment! I looked at my phone quickly and saw that my friend had now texted a reply to my cheeky message of a few hours ago. Whatever she had said, it was too late now, which was a bit unfortunate because what she says is: 'NO WAY! NEVER TAKE CLIENTS TO MY HOUSE, WHAT ARE YOU THINKING???'

As you might expect, the blood drained out of not only my face. The lesbians looked at me and suggested cutting the session short. I agreed and it was clear to see that we were all hugely relieved. Once I had hurried the women out as quickly as possible, I erased any possible evidence from the sheets of any of us ever having been there. I never told my friend. I felt she'd be happier not knowing. So let's keep this story between ourselves.

You see the sex life of an escort isn't quite what you might think it is. How great, most men would think, to be paid by two good-looking lesbians to teach them how to have sex with a man! It's *Emmanuel* and then some! The premise sounds sexy, but the reality? Less so. But you know what, that particular encounter, if not sexy, was really human and basic and friendly and awkward and humorous and touching. That's not so bad for a morning's work.

Some of my work is like that. Some of it is more unpleasant and coarse, but then I have been lucky enough to have had encounters and experiences which are wonderfully meaningful and made me feel as if I was doing something worthwhile and significant. For example, I have obese and very old clients. Neither of those things bothers me in the slightest in terms of my work. In fact, I prefer it to some fabulous looker who thinks I should be grateful to have sex with them and offer them my services for free. But working with someone who has trouble finding sexual fulfilment in their day-to-day lives I find extremely satisfying.

One of my regular clients is seventy-two years old and worked for years in a senior position in the civil service. She's an extremely civilized person, well off, and mainly all she wants to do is talk or for us to go out to supper together. Her husband of many years died fifteen years ago and she says she came across my ad by accident in the back pages of a satirical magazine. I'm thrilled that in some way I can help her still feel in touch with her sexuality. Eroticism doesn't just wither away with age for many people, but it can be hard nurturing that side if you're left alone. I'm more than happy to help, because doing sex stuff with someone old is actually really interesting, and you can learn a lot about the human body by getting naked with someone your grandmother's age – skin gets softer as well as more wrinkled and older people have a distinctive, though not unpleasant, scent to them.

Sometimes, when I am arousing her by kissing her or putting my fingers in her pussy, she says, 'This is a sin, isn't it, Andrew?' She knows all about my background in the Church because she is one of the few clients I have frank conversations with; most of our time together is spent in conversation. 'I don't think so,' I respond, 'but what do you think? That's what's important.' She pauses and then responds to her own question. 'In many ways the definition of this kind of sin is in the eyes of the beholder. In one sense sin can be seen as absolute, but don't you think God is more fluid and forgiving when it comes to times like these, when no one is being hurt or abused?' After one session she said something particularly poignant to me. 'At my age, Andrew, one of the things you miss most is being held and having your hair stroked. Sex is the long way round to a cuddle.'

I was moved when she said this to me, and I felt grateful for being young and able-bodied. It felt good to be able to do something for her, something that made her feel connected to the world, made her look forward to the next time we saw each other. Sometimes elderly people can go for months without being touched – just think, weeks and weeks and weeks without a kind touch, how isolating that must be, and how sad – and in that way I hope I helped her. In another session not long afterwards she told me that she had been to the doctor, who had told her that her blood pressure had dropped. She attributed this wholly to my attentions.

I also have the honour of working with disabled people and they have taught me a great deal. Obviously everything takes longer if you are not able-bodied, from getting up the stairs to getting dressed and undressed, never mind building up trust, but I gain something much more valuable from this work. The most important lesson I learnt was that disabled people are exactly the same as everybody else. I knew that in my head, but it was news to me sexually. Of course they've got the same desires and longings – from fancying George Clooney or the lead singer in a boy band to wishing for intimacy or wanting to experiment or test their boundaries and live out their fantasies – as anyone else.

I became involved with an agency called Tender Loving Care, a non-profit organization that catered for disabled people who have no access to sex, or believe they haven't, other than through a charity and an escort. One of the clients an agency sent me was blind. Before she came over she called me on the telephone to make sure I knew about her disability. She actually apologized to me for it. 'Oh please,' I said. 'That makes no difference to me at all, as long as you feel comfortable.'

'It won't be a problem to you?' she asked, again.

'It's fine,' I said. ' Just come along. Come now if it suits you. It's totally fine.'

She was a small, slight woman, with beautiful pale skin and reddish hair that she wore tucked behind her ears. She was very attractive, in a quiet sort of way, and seemed shy. I asked her a few questions and I could tell that the short answers she gave me were more through nerves than anything else. I led her into my bedroom. I had pulled the curtains and lit scented candles – I thought she might appreciate the smell – if she couldn't see then I was going to try and fill up the rest of her senses. 'I'm nervous,' she confided to me.

'That's fine,' I whispered, as I touched the side of her cheek. 'Sometimes I'm nervous too.'

I led her to the bed and she sat down. 'The room smells nice,' she said.

I put on some music, something quiet, to set the mood. 'Let me help you with your clothes,' I said.

I took off her shoes and rolled her pantyhose down, all the while whispering to her, telling her how delicate and fine her feet were, kissing the arch of her foot and moving up her leg, planting kisses as I travelled north.

'Wait,' she said, 'I'd like to feel you.'

I quickly slipped out of my clothes and helped her get out of the rest of hers. Then she touched me, her fingers at times feather soft, at others hard, feeling the muscles of my chest and my stomach before finding their way to my cock, which was now very hard at her expert touch. 'It's been such a long time,' she whispered.

She started to stroke me, while I caressed her small, soft breasts. She let out a moan when I bent down and sucked her nipple. I moved my lips up to the nape of her neck. 'I should be the one pleasing you,' I said, and took her to the bed again, where I laid her down.

She may have begun the session quietly, but after I went down on her, her moans and groans got louder and louder. 'I want you inside me,' she begged. 'Please.'

But I took my time, teasing her now flushed skin with the tips of my fingers. Her skin was so sensitive after she had come that she was moaning and writhing on the bed with pleasure at my touch. 'Please,' she said, 'please, fuck me.'

We fucked each other. It was so intense, her beautiful fingers fluttering over my face, clutching my shoulders and finally digging into my back when she had her second orgasm.

One of my favourite disabled clients is a Spanish woman called Caterina. Caterina's legs are amputated below the knee, and she has spent most of her life on sticks or in a wheelchair. When I first met her she was extremely shy. She could handle her disability well – she had a good job and was without any bitterness at all, she was utterly lovely as a person in fact – but her self-esteem in terms of men and sex was at an all-time low. It didn't take me long to discern (and she more or less let me know) that she had been badly treated by her father and subsequently by men in general. She told me bluntly that she'd never come close to an orgasm.

When we first spoke by phone before we met she said, 'I'm so nervous. I'm frightened I might bottle it and stand you up and I don't want to waste your time.'

'I'm willing to risk it,' I said. 'And you can always come over and still not do anything. We could just have a cup of tea. There's no pressure at all. I might get nervous too! Would you mind that?' I think that reassured her and indeed one afternoon she got in a cab, came over from Streatham, and didn't bottle it.

The first thing she wanted to do, she told me, was learn how to give a blow job.

'I've done it before,' she said. 'When I was in my late teens and early twenties I had a couple of boyfriends over the years but whenever I gave them a blow job they said I was terrible at it, so I lost my confidence.' When Caterina told me that, I wanted to kill those men. OK, so her blow job wasn't great at first but only really because her mouth was at the wrong angle to my cock. That was easily solved by me being more proactive and changing my position. Kneeling in front of her worked much better and after a few attempts her rhythm too got much better. So much about sex is to do with confidence.

After that I taught her how to put on a condom. How

does one know, disabled or not, that the teat on a condom should be pushed out otherwise air gets in and the condom might break?

We practised condom expertise for a long time and by the end of our sessions she could do it perfectly and with her mouth only! Trust me, if you have to use a condom it helps sex up the whole experience if you can put one on using only your mouth. All it takes is practice.

Caterina came to see me for a long afternoon every three weeks for six months. We arranged a special rate for our sessions, but I know they still cost her a great deal in many other ways, because she took an afternoon off from work when a weekend wasn't possible if I was away visiting my family or on a stag weekend with the football boys. Plus taxis from Streatham to central London don't come cheap for people who are often on benefits.

She was always beautifully turned out and made up, her body smelling fresh and lightly perfumed. I appreciated the care she put into preparing for me. We always had tea and sometimes champagne when she arrived and always talked for a long time before getting down to 'work'. Even getting Caterina up the stairs required quite a lot of effort and I tried to make it into a special journey with sit-downs for both of us after each set of stairs, plus we both used humour as well as affection to calm our nerves. I'd stroke her hair to calm her down and relax her while we chatted, and then when it came to getting undressed I might say something along the lines of: 'Can I help you take off your jumper? Your bra? ... Your legs?'

Quite often I had to turn down a lucrative job because Caterina was coming to see me, but it was always worth it. I'll never forget the first time she came, after she gave me a blow job and I said to her, 'Why don't I go down on you now? I'd like to if you're up for it,' and though she was nervous, she said why not. Listen, I was nervous as hell too. After all, the pressure is on. If Caterina can't get an orgasm from the 'expert' then she's going to think *she's a failure*. She's worrying anyway that she is incapable of it, which isn't going to relax her, and if I can't get her off it's going to compound her worse fears. But all I could do was take my own advice: relax, try to get into the zone, calm down and enjoy myself while listening and feeling for her responses too. And she did respond; her release and pleasure were certainly real. I was struck by a feeling that this was a magical moment in life because I had been a source of healing, of wonder and of real progression. It's not often you get to say that in any profession and it's not what people automatically assume a prostitute provides when he or she is paid for sex, but you know what, it just shows how little any of us can assume, and how wondrous and powerful sex can be.

CHAPTER 10

Work Of Art - For Sale

My professional life was going well – there was no doubt about that. It was now 2002, and I had had wonderful experiences, and less wonderful ones: the no-shows, the bargainers, the collectors and the saviours. Most of my work was what I'd call fairly bread-and-butter sessions, and though my day included runs to my Selfridges cash box with envelopes of cash and often having an early morning breakfast at my favourite café after an all-nighter, it was also made up of the more mundane tasks we all have to get done: phone calls, grocery shopping, going to the gym – like any sex worker you can be planning all these things in your head while still performing.

A bread-and-butter session might be as simple as servicing one of my regular female clients. Apart from Caterina, I have a number of women clients I see fairly often – Cheryl of course (though there is nothing bread and butter about working with *her*), Stripogram Woman and Witchy all stand out for different reasons.

Stripogram Woman didn't perform raunchy dances in a nurse's outfit herself, but was enamoured by the Chippendale-type guy and the strip routine. Her fantasy was to woo and save 'a lost boy'. I wasn't mad about her, but she's a good enough customer, though not kind. She's single, wealthy, in her mid to late forties and she had a lot of confidence in some ways and none at all in others. A bad Jewish-American girl living in North London, she knows what she wants but is always trying to get something extra for nothing. She wants to save me – but I don't need saving.

She has a high-profile job in a man's world, and dresses and behaves like a power woman. In her professional life she is very successful but when it comes to handling men in her personal life she is hopeless. She is fairly overweight, which I don't mind about in the slightest, but I think it adds to her insecurities and is just one part of the reason she is mixed up when it comes to sex. Or maybe it works the other way round. You're mixed up about sex and so you add a few layers of protection to your body. I don't know. All I do know is that she can't be straightforward, even with me, when things should have been clear-cut.

One of the problems has always been that she fancies the much younger guys she employs and feels rejected by the fact that they don't want to go out with her – I suspect she may come on a bit strong towards them and I've tried to tell her not to take it so personally. Very few young guys in their late teens or early twenties on the make want to go out with a woman who is over twenty-five years older than them and their boss to boot. But that's what she likes about me. I could be one of her employees or her fantasy stripper – though I promise you the fantasy is better than the reality and trust me when I tell you I'm the worst dancer on the planet.

'You just say the word, Andrew,' she would say, 'and I'll sort you out. You can move in if you like.' But anyway, that wasn't ever the point. The point is I've never really believed her. I've been promised the world by clients over the years. I've been promised cars, houses and to be set up in my own business. But it's not as simple as that, I've learnt. My time may be for sale, but I'm not.

People often hire escorts who match, as much as possible, the object of their fantasy. Maybe it's someone who looks like their secretary or their headmaster or a current pop star. Stripogram Woman, for example, assumed that because I embodied, or partly embodied, her fantasy, the feeling must be reciprocal. Of course I don't think she really, rationally thought this, but sex and desire isn't rational. She used to want to barter with me, instead of simply paying my standard, agreed fee.

We'd meet in a boutique hotel – the Sanderson, say – and she'd say, 'Andrew, anything you want to buy. Anything you want to eat or drink. Champagne by the bucketload. Let's do it and then let's just have fun together and forget about the other stuff.' I was quite firm with her, and in an odd way I think that's actually why she liked me. But then no one seemed ever to say to her, yes, darling, yes I want to be with you, yes I love you, yes let's have fun together. I had to explain that gifts are all well and good but it's cash that counts. Profit is sanity, gifts a vanity.

One job I had involved me taking a taxi way out of central London to a small bedsit in an anonymous suburb west of London. I knew that my client was young, but I was amazed to find a stunning eighteen-year-old letting me into her flat up about a million flights of stairs. She was an Arab-Israeli, she told me, and working in London as a model. She found me on a website and had saved up for a session specially. She handed me my fee as a handful of crumpled ten-pound notes. Her flatmates, two students, were out, she said, but we couldn't make too much noise because she didn't know when one of them might come back. 'You're gorgeous,' I said to her. She was. 'What are you doing this for? Hiring me. If you're after sex you could get it anywhere for free.'

She explained that her boyfriend, whom she loved, was Muslim, and that he was abstaining from sex during Ramadan. 'That's quite a long time for me,' she said, and though she was being frank, I could tell that she was also very shy. 'Too long. I guess you could say I'm highly sexed and I thought this would be fun. This way it doesn't feel like I'm betraying my boyfriend.' This is definitely an interpretation of the holy fast of Ramadan that I've not heard of before! Still, for someone so up front in her talk she was remarkably shy in bed. She wasn't stiff exactly, but she made no forward moves at all. When I kissed her, she would respond and kiss me back but it took a long time for her arms or hands to start to wander over my body or touch me. I began to undress her slowly, caressing her all the time. She seemed pleased and made soft sighs of satisfaction, but when I began undressing myself I could see that she was so shy she couldn't really look at my naked body. 'What turns you on?' I asked her, as I had the feeling that she'd only really been used to pleasing men, rather than telling them what worked for her. 'What would you like me to do to you?'

'Whatever you like,' she replied quietly. 'What do you like?'

'I like you,' I said to her, which was true. 'I like your beautiful body and your beautiful skin and your beautiful soft breasts.' I knew that she liked me kissing and licking her breasts because she arched her back towards me and began to run her hands down my back, but I could also tell that she was still inhibited, which I found charming. I took her over to her bed and gently laid her down. I spent a long time just touching her all over her body with my fingers and tongue and when I felt that she was ready I gently inserted my fingers into her pussy, asking her in a whisper at the same time if this was all right.

'Are you ready?' I asked. 'Is this what you want?' She nodded and kissed my neck in response, pulling me closer to her, but not once did she touch my cock. I entered her gently in the missionary position, and began to move slowly inside her. She responded by moving her hips in time with mine. I spent a long time inside her, trying, carefully, to build her up to a climax. She seemed to enjoy it. I like to think so anyway and by the end her sighs increased to moans and her moans became louder until she seemed, I think, to come and experience a huge release of pleasure and energy. I don't think she was faking it, but I am not presumptuous enough to say for sure. 'Shall I come inside you?' I asked her once she had climaxed. (Obviously, I was wearing a condom.) 'Yes,' she said. 'Yes. Come inside me. I want you to come inside me.' It was the most she had said since we had started touching, but it felt incredibly intimate and trusting. I came hard and with my own strong shudders.

She was lovely, that young woman, and a few follow-up texts followed that session – I think I was hoping that she'd want to see more of me, and not merely in a professional capacity, but no, her texts were merely polite responses to my own and she never called me again. The thing was, now that Hannah and I had parted, I hadn't had anyone special in my life for a long time and I felt intensely lonely.

I was so attracted to the Israeli model that I think I projected my hopes of something more coming out of it on to her, much like the Croupier or the Stripogram Woman had projected their needs on to me. The irony was I had the opportunity to sleep with all these amazing women, but I had no real woman of my own.

Even if a relationship crossed over into sugar mummy and sugar boy it would still be highly defined, if not paid strictly by the hour. We would still have our roles to play, and the moment one of us might forget that is the moment things would start to go wrong. But I've never come close to finding a sugar mummy and never wanted to give that much away anyway, quite frankly. I'd rather continue to hire bits of myself out by the hour and remain in control of my time, than commit myself to one person for the sake of money.

If very occasionally I have to remind myself of my role in respect of the women I work with, as with the Israeli model, it is more often that I have to remind my clients. Another regular at this time was Witchy. Witchy, a middle-aged woman who shops and is into new-age crystals, Native American spirituality, that sort of thing, found me through one of my ads on the back of her local newspaper. I always quite relished advertising in this paper because it is a conservative publication that condemns prostitution on its front pages, while surviving off the profits it makes from the very same prostitutes who pay its specially inflated advertising rates on the back pages. If you're a man with a van and want to advertise in this paper the price is one level, but it is sixteen times higher if you are an escort, even though you are using exactly the same size box for your advertisement.

Witchy told me she was a witch when she first came to see me in my Pimlico flat. She also described herself as a pagan and a wicca. Basically she was big into crystals and spells. That was fine by me as long as she was happy to pay me. And she could pay. She was secretive about where she lived – I didn't particularly want to know the details anyway and was just trying to make small talk – but I got the feeling that she was hiding secrets from me. Nothing sinister, just the fact that she was well off, lived in a large house in some fancy part of London and was married. She told me she wasn't married, but somehow I just felt she was. Again, it's not really any of my business and doesn't bother me either way; it was more that I was curious about why she was so intent on hiding the fact from me.

Still, whatever her real-life situation was, she seemed to have plenty of time to see me and plenty of cash to pay for that time. Sometimes she booked me for an hour but mainly she wanted an overnight session in my flat. Witchy definitely came to me for sex – she likes being taken from behind quite hard and fast, and sometimes for a long, long time. She also liked a lot of foreplay and for me to go down on her for as long as possible. I know this is my job and I'm happy to oblige, but sometimes my enthusiasm wanes when I have to do it for so, so long. 'Don't stop,' Witchy would say when I was going down on her, and I wouldn't, but after half an hour of eating her out I would begin to get lockjaw and feel short of oxygen. Even if I put my head up for a bit of air she would push me back down and say, 'Not yet. I'm not there yet.' It took a long, long time and a great deal of licking and fucking to get her there, believe me. But as well as lots of sex, it's companionship of the boyfriend-girlfriend type that she was after when she spent the night with me. This made me more uncomfortable than having to get a second erection hot on the heels of a first one, but I played along with it – up to a point.

For example, Witchy was interested in star signs and she regularly tried to read my fortune, but because escorts are always fibbing about their age (they are always older than they claim to be), I gave her my wrong birth date. She brought me crystals to put round my bed too – I'm not quite sure what she expected them to do – but she expected something. As she performed her crystal rituals I'd just say, 'That's lovely. Thank you.'

We talked a lot. Or rather she talked and I listened. I knew she wasn't telling me everything about her background or circumstances, but she did reveal some stuff, such as the fact that she had a second home in Cornwall in a village near the one where I grew up, though of course she didn't know that. But my antennae went up and I knew, to my bones, the places she spoke about so romantically. And boy, did she romanticize the West Country. Of course it is beautiful in Cornwall, and of course much of the landscape is powerful and mysterious, but she truly believes it is a place filled with practical, real magic, if that isn't a contradiction in terms.

But then so much was magical and spiritual to Witchy. She didn't just have an orgasm with me, it was a 'special experience like a waterfall flowing over the mountain paths and stars colliding in the sky'. She sent me parcels after each session containing soft toys like Forever Friends teddy bears. I built up quite a collection of them. The cards she sent with the teddies were the kind that young girls tend to buy for their school friends. You know the ones with bubbly writing all over them and warm messages printed inside. The problem is, I don't want a collection of Forever Friends teddies. To me, they are junk cluttering up my flat, and yet I can't take them down to the Oxfam shop because Witchy expects to see them nesting happily together on my bed, the bed that she expects to be for ever protected by the crystals she has given me.

She wanted to share things with me. Not just stories or crystals or teddy bears either, but experiences and, even more inappropriate (not to mention impossible for me), *feelings*. My favourite gift from her, the one that actually made me laugh out loud when it arrived, was a clod of Cornwall earth. Yes, a lump of earth, about four centimetres square, that arrived in a box wrapped up with reused brown paper and a lot of information about how we are all connected to the earth, with references to Celtic stuff linked to Native American Indians.

I longed to be able to phone my brother or one of my friends from back home so that I could say: 'You'll never guess what, this lady has sent me some earth from just down the road from us, with a whole story of spirituality about mother earth and our connection to the soil and who we are as people.' But I couldn't, of course, because they knew nothing about my life in escorting. And here's a real cost, whether you have a funny story to tell like a clod of earth sent to you as a gift, or were just given a £5000 tip or felt threatened in some way: there's no one to tell and that's the price you pay, a dividend in social isolation.

There's no real moral to my story of Witchy, except that what she expected from me, I could never give her, and so our 'arrangement' finally came to an end. She wanted me to be in love with her but she couldn't ignore the facts for ever. I didn't feign interest in her choices of conversation. I never faked any feelings for her. And that shows, even in the sex we had together. I didn't really want to make love for hours with her.

After a while I stopped making an effort in terms of our

sex together, which was frankly unprofessional of me, and as a result she began to see me less and less. But you know what? That was fine with me. Some clients you cherish, some are important and others you have to let fall by the wayside. The last straw came when she called me and asked to come over for an hour's session as soon as possible. I agreed because I was free and it would only be an hour after all, but I was caught somewhat unprepared and I forgot to lay out the crystals and arrange the soft toys and I think the clod of earth had long since gone into my window boxes. That was when the penny finally dropped for her. It must have been horrible for her, I'm sure, to realize that, for me, she was just a client, whereas she had been investing all this time and energy in me, thinking about me when we weren't together, thinking of my face when she gave me a Forever Friends bear or a crystal that had healing properties. And she must have felt humiliated when she realized that I had been only tolerating her attentions, rather than looking forward to them. When I saw her face – the realization that I was no more than an escort and she was just a client was plain to see – I felt a pang of guilt at being so harsh towards her. But her obsession with me wasn't healthy – not for her, not for me – and it had to end at some point, and unfortunately it ended that day. She didn't call me again.

There was someone who was calling me most days though and not for professional matters. Hannah.

Although I was thoroughly enjoying living on my own in London and didn't miss my Cambridge life at all, there was something grounding and comforting about hearing Hannah's voice on the phone, and I realized that on the days she didn't call, I'd miss her. It took me a while to wake up to this, and I didn't ever call her myself, but I did wonder if the reason I hadn't dated any girls for longer than a couple of nights might have something to do with some residual feelings for Hannah. I didn't have to wonder for too long. Circumstances transpired that we had to meet up again.

What happened was this. The tax man caught up with me. Between 2002 and 2003 I was investigated by the Inland Revenue. My beautiful cash business, which I had enjoyed so freely for five years, had run its course and it was time to face up to what I owed and how I would handle my affairs in the future. I decided to come completely clean and tell the tax man everything. I came clean not only about my financial affairs and how I hadn't exactly paid tax for five years, but also about exactly what I did for a living and why I had been operating a cash business for so long. I went into considerable details, even revealing some of the actual nature of my work, such as roleplays and dressing up.

You try keeping a straight face when you're dressed up as Superman with a client whose ultimate fantasy is to be Lois Lane, and a Lois Lane who has defected to the dark side and has to have her wicked way after sapping Superman's strength with her own precious stash of kryptonite. You have to take such requests seriously at the time, and in fact I find harmless fantasies such as this perfectly endearing, plus my client could have a laugh about it with me – yes, it was what turned her on, but that didn't preclude humour from our sessions – so I thought it only fair to include such stories in my report, along with how much I'd pocketed from such a job. I thought, well, I might as well make this as exciting as possible for whoever is auditing my case. My aim was to at least put a smile on the investigating officer's face.

It worked. In the end, it seemed, the tax office were fairly lenient with me. I had to pay my back taxes of course (and a large sum at that), and a fine, but the fine didn't break me and, of course, I'd benefited from spending what I should have been paying in tax on deposits for houses. In the end I was philosophical. I saw paying my back taxes as paying back a loan, a loan I'd done well from.

The IR investigation, as well as sorting my finances out, had two other extremely significant consequences. One joyful (though ultimately painful), the other pretty torturous. The good thing that happened was that it led to Hannah and I reuniting. I didn't want to draw Hannah into the investigation I was under, but given her previous involvement in managing my properties, I felt I should let her know what was going on. We agreed to meet. I was ambivalent about this, probably because I knew that Hannah was eager to give things another go. I felt less sure and I didn't want to meet her only to reject her. I was also worried that if we did meet then any dormant feelings I had for her, which though I tried to deny it I couldn't quite extinguish, would flourish back into life. I was busy. I was making a lot of money. I fancied Innocence and we'd just started doing duos together that sometimes felt more like the real thing.

I remember the first time I saw Innocence naked. I thought, this girl is a pro. I could understand why, once you'd seen Innocence, you didn't mind paying her sky-high prices. No wonder she could afford all her luxuries with ease. Every inch of her was toned, tight, polished, scrubbed and softened. She was hairless in all the right places but hadn't taken it to naked extremes with her pussy. She was also an expert in bed and seemed to be able to sense exactly what you wanted next – how fast, how slow, how soft, how hard – before even you'd realized it yourself. And so, for many reasons, I didn't want to get back into a serious relationship at this time of my life. Did I?

It seemed that I did. The moment I saw Hannah, waiting for me in a café near my flat, I knew I was still in love with her. Or at least that's how it felt. Maybe we were both lonely and looking for love and it was easy to fall for each other again. Or maybe it was something more? Maybe we were actually meant to be – it certainly felt that way. And no one knew me like Hannah, no one had been through so much with me, no one had ever understood me like she did. Not that any of my friends understood. My brother couldn't believe it. The first thing my best friend Catherine said when I told her was: 'You must be joking! You two? I thought living together had been a disaster.' She was right. It had. But it seemed we were both willing to try it again. We'd both work harder at it, we promised each other. And we also had another idea: not to live together for a while, but instead to sell some of our individual houses – the property market in 2003 was at a fantastic high – buy a house together in London, bank any spare funds, rent out the new house and go travelling together for nine months. My brother was ominously quiet when I told him our plans, never a good sign.

It took us quite a long time to find what we were looking for in London. It was easy as anything to sell my tiny studio, but find a large, centrally located flat with the right configuration of rooms so that we could both work at the same time and have our own untouchable bedroom and space? It was hard, but we finally found, towards the end of 2003, a wonderfully large and light three-bedroom duplex with a large sitting room and proper, spacious hallway (important for letting clients in and out, with the added advantage that you never have to go through one room to get to another, which means all rooms can be in operation at the same time without any risk of interruption) in St James's.

The apparent downside was that the people who owned the flat were both desperate to sell and unable to move (they were in their own house-buying chain), but in fact this suited us down to the ground. We weren't ready to live there anyway, and needed to rent it out so that we could spend freely while travelling, so for the flat to come with ready-made tenants was perfect. Of course we didn't know quite how long they'd be there and we couldn't ask them to sign a lease, but that didn't worry us too much – we'd cross that bridge when we came to it – and more crucially Hannah used this as a bargaining chip in negotiations and managed to knock a fifth off their asking price.

The flat is located in a conservation area in a grade-two listed building near Trafalgar Square, and I love it. It's close to the area where Nell Gwyn used to live and work as a prostitute, and where she met the Prince of Wales who was to become Charles the Second. 'Our Nell' the Londoners of her day liked to call her.

'Pretty Witty Nell', as Samuel Pepys referred to her, was born in 1650, the daughter of a brothel owner, and of course worked as a prostitute herself before becoming the king's favourite mistress and a famous actress of her day. In fact, that's how she met the king – to this day the Earl of Burford and the Duke of St Albans have hereditary titles because of their union.

I'm particularly fond of Nell Gwyn and her story and love living in her neighbourhood. I find it amazing there is no statue commemorating her extraordinary life. The more I find out about the history of London's sex workers, the more fascinated I become by it – and the more appalled by the age-long hypocrisy that has always surrounded, and still does alas, every aspect of it. It's not just Nell Gwyn that has no statue, for example. There is no plaque at all in London, anywhere, commemorating anything to do with the sex industry, and yet it's the oldest profession there is.

I've loved the life in Central London. You can meet all kinds of people on every street corner, or in any of the bars or clubs or pubs that crowd the area. There is always a good party going on within walking distance of my house – the sort of parties where you meet beautiful women who know how to enjoy themselves. It was at one such party where I met Little Miss Party. Miss Party is not an escort and never has been, but she is the sort of girl who is constantly given expensive gifts by men, often men she hardly knows or who have just met her. She seems to have that sort of effect on men: she is so sexy and in such a warm way that men want to offer themselves up to her, and because it's hard to do that without making a fool of yourself, they buy her presents instead.

I recently ran into Little Miss Party in Bond Street where she was returning a £1000 paperweight she'd been given, which was of no use to her, in exchange for a juicy credit note. I know that the idea of being a high-class escort has occurred to Miss Party – she knows escorts and sees how much money the really good ones can make – but the thing about Miss Party is that she has something different about her. She is young and beautiful and gifted: at a party she's the one who will stand up on a table and rap in time to a backbeat or dance to a groove or sing a ballad.

She can do anything, it seems, and really she should be putting her energy into becoming a recording artist or a superstar or whatever it is that she wants to be, and not fall back into something she knows she can do easily and which of course she'd be good at. How do I know? Because Miss Party and I found ourselves at a loose end after a night out and decided to continue having fun, just ourselves and a few close friends. It was pretty wild. As an escort, I don't usually allow myself to go all out when I'm with clients – although getting a little drunk on the job is fine, getting wasted is an absolute no-no, but that night I let rip. We ordered bottle after bottle of Cristal, ordered on Little Miss Party's rich suitor's account, of course, and drank them all. I remember Little Miss Party accidentally pouring champagne down the front of her dress and me and her best friend licking it off. People were snogging in corners, the music was loud, tacky and hugely enjoyable, and the sun came up the next day without any of us noticing that the night had passed; we felt elated.

The next day when she'd gone, I found myself saying a

short prayer for her. 'Dear Father, I pray that you will look after Miss Party. She has so many exciting and wonderful things ahead of her and I know instinctively that she will succeed in whatever it is she wants to do. I ask that she will never become an escort. She has much more important things to do with her life.'

But this part of London isn't just about the people you meet in the bars and clubs and cafés. The places themselves are often like characters in their own right. I love it that if I turn right and walk for a minute or two there is Balans restaurant on Old Compton Street, a haunt for many escorts, as well as actors and musicians and anyone who leads a night life, simply because it serves food until very late. You won't find a waiter hovering over you at 11 p.m. because the kitchen is closing, and believe me, if you work odd hours or late into the night, that's a relief, whatever your trade. Mind you, you pay – full whack London prices – for this luxury. But in the opposite direction to Balans, but just as close, is what would come to be another favourite haunt, the Chandos Café.

I love the Chandos for its unpretentious clientele, so different from the performers and night-life lovers who inhabit Balans. Basically, the Chandos is a police and theatre worker's café (it's right opposite Charing Cross police station). If I need to eat late I go to Balans, but if I need to eat really, really late then it's a six o'clock breakfast at the Chandos, along with various policemen and women, both in and out of uniform, either ending or just beginning their shifts.

It sounds glamorous, in a TV drama kind of way, doesn't it? Prostitutes and coppers getting their fuel before or after working the busy streets of London. But guess what, when I stumble in there bleary-eyed and often a little drunk after a night shift of my own, it's not eventful or glamorous in the least. There's no drama in the Chandos. It's just filled with hard workers drinking coffee, keeping their heads down and eating their eggs, bacon and toast.

Hannah and I bought our house, situated as it is wonderfully close to all these places, in our joint names, but it was me who put down the deposit, me who paid the considerable stamp duty and me who took out the mortgage, which, although it's covered by rent as long as our tenants stay in it, I am ultimately responsible for. But I don't care about any of this when we buy our St James's pad. I love it. I love everything about it. But we don't properly discover the daily delights that surround living in such a hub until we return from our travels abroad and settle into our London life together.

Only of course everything couldn't be quite as smooth as silk. Not when you're an escort. The HMRC investigation had brought me and Hannah back together again and this seemed a fantastic thing, but it also, inadvertently, led to someone dark and sinister entering my life. Just as Hannah and I were making plans to go abroad, to forget about escorting and work and enjoy our youth, earnings and freedom, I was being squeezed tightly and horribly by an accountant who had decided to blackmail me. And if I thought I could take on anyone who threatened me in such a way, it was because until this moment I hadn't encountered a real expert.

CHAPTER 11

Madness Becomes Normality In Our House

We should have been having the time of our lives. In ten months Hannah and I took twenty-five flights and travelled in five continents. We hiked in the Andes and scuba-dived in the Bahamas. We bungee-jumped in New Zealand and went on safari in Tanzania. That's not the only thing we did in that beautiful country, either. We got engaged. It wasn't quite a bended-knee moment, but it was romantic for all that. We were sitting on the shores of Lake Victoria, the sun was setting and the time seemed right. I had been building up to this moment throughout our trip. 'Hannah,' I said, taking her hands in mine. 'I love you, will you marry me?' Perhaps now, in hindsight, I could say that I noticed some hesitation in her eyes, but that may just be hindsight talking. She did say yes, and I hugged her to me. It really felt like this trip was going to mark a turning point in our lives.

It was an amazing time. Magical. But it was also tainted by the fact that I was being blackmailed by the accountant I had signed on. After all, I was now straight financially and in order to stay that way I needed a professional to help me file my tax returns and keep my accounts in perfect order.

The problem was, I compromised on finding the right professional. My accountant was qualified all right: it's just that she was also a client of mine. I met her through a mortgage broker who specialized in helping escorts find mortgages – escorts often have difficulty getting financial services even though they can earn a high and steady income – and our deal was that we would swap services. I would still receive bills, but they would be much lower than normal. Could I have had a worse idea? It turned out I couldn't.

The first problem is that doing business with clients, like doing business with friends, can spiral out of control, and because you have taken things out of a strictly professional realm, there is little you can do to rein things back in. My client/accountant, for instance, took for ever to sort out any of my accounts and when she did finally get round to it I could see she'd done a sloppy job. That meant that when she came calling, I didn't much feel like putting a lot of effort into pleasing her. I didn't feel like it at all, and I told her that, no, she wouldn't be getting any more from me. What I was trying to do was assert myself, but you can't assert yourself properly from a position of inherent weakness, of exposure.

The fact is, I needed professionalism from her far more than she needed it from me, and I should have realized this. I am so strict about keeping so much of my life carefully separated from escorting, and yet here I was, blurring a very important boundary. It didn't work. Don't do it. Why did I? Greed, I suppose, and the feeling that I was invincible.

I should never have played with this particular fire. Days after refusing the accountant sex, I received an extremely large bill for her services. Clearly, she was teaching me a lesson. She was in her early forties, rather self-important, very successful – and unused to compromise. She spent hours each week in the gym and doing yoga classes, and she owned a yacht with her partner. Certainly, she wasn't used to rejection and wasn't going to let such a thing go lightly. Days after the first bill, another one, equally large, arrived. And days after that a third. Then a fourth. All carefully post-date reconstructed. It became clear that I was not merely being charged for her services but being blackmailed. After all, she charges by the hour but after a short period of time my bills equalled £34,000.

I tried to fight back. I asked her for a breakdown of her bill so that she could explain such a colossal figure. I contacted the sex workers' branch of the GMB union and they told me they had access to solicitors who would help me. They encouraged me to take her on, only to drop the case midway through, much to my frustration and disappointment. With hindsight, of course, I wish I'd just fucked her and paid off the first bill for £15,000. But I took the union's advice and trusted them to back me up. It was a bitter disappointment to see its solicitors apparently so lacking.

It didn't help that Hannah and I were on the other side of the world while this business was escalating and the figure was rising. Wherever we went, I had to find an internet café, while dreading what I was going to find in my inbox. Mostly it was nothing. Mostly she didn't respond to my emails and long-distance telephone calls, but if anything her silence, accompanied by more bills, was even less bearable.

Eventually, I was forced to capitulate. She began sending paperwork to my parents' house, so showing herself to be a very sinister threat to me. Who could I go to in such a situation? Not the police. Not the union, it turned out. Jonny Bedlam was very willing to do something to help, but that's a path I've never wanted to go down.

I transferred the money into the accountant's bank account and never heard from her again. I was furious for allowing myself to get into a situation where I could be so easily manipulated. What a needlessly expensive way to learn a lesson. But then, just as you think you know every-thing, something else comes along to prove things otherwise. I am philosophical now about the £34,000 I paid to that accountant. I have to be.

Back to the good news. Hannah and I were engaged! I remember before asking her to marry me having this very conscious, clear thought, that Hannah really was the one. That this was it. That my future was now, in many respects, set and that this would be a wonderful thing. I had found my mate. I would no longer be making my way in the world alone. Instead, I would look after Hannah and she would look after me and our lives would be forever intertwined. Together we came up with a plan for our future.

Once we returned from travelling, we would get married. We'd hopefully be able to move into the house we'd bought together (our tenants seemed to be resolving their own house-buying traumas and looked like they'd be moving on at a time that might suit us perfectly). Using the house we'd bought as base, we'd both work for a time. Hannah would run the housing business – though we'd sold some of our properties to buy our London place, we still owned six or seven properties between us, and managed a handful more for other people – while I would continue to escort. I'd work from home in an area separate from our untouchable matrimonial quarters upstairs.

Two years, we reckoned, of working hard would secure our future, and in April 2006, at the end of the tax year,

I planned to officially retire from the business of selling sex. Then, so we planned, we would have children. Hannah would become a housewife and full-time mother, which is what she said she really wanted to be, and I would take over running the housing business, which under Hannah's watchful and by now experienced eye would have flourished and grown. When the housing market in central London felt like it couldn't possibly get any higher, we'd cash in our London chips, sell the flat and bugger off to wherever took our fancy, then settle into the life of having children. I knew that I would eventually have to swap the high-paced world of the sex worker, with all its risks and pleasures, for one that was less dramatic, but also less superficial. At least that was the plan.

All this was ahead of me, though, when Hannah and I were in Australia, newly engaged and happy, yes, but still fighting. But everyone fights when they are travelling and together 24/7. Don't they? And we had huge amounts of fun too. Hannah encouraged me to do things I would not have done without her, whether it was swimming with dolphins, bungee-jumping or getting up while it was still dark to witness the sun rising.

We weren't entirely carefree, however. I had my blackmailing accountant to deal with and Hannah was in constant touch with my brother over the housing business. She wasn't happy with the job he was doing, and told me she thought he was overcharging her for certain things, repairs and the like. But my brother would never ever try to skim off any money from anyone and least of all his future sister-in-law, I argued. If he isn't doing the absolute best job running the business, I told her, then that is probably because he didn't want to do the job in the first place. Now I look back on those months together and can see some of our behaviour as warning signs of what lay ahead, but back then I didn't want to know about warning signs and nor did Hannah. Instead we put any problems we were having down to the fact that we were together so much and shared such an isolating secret about my job.

We returned from our travels in May 2004. Our wedding was planned for that coming July, which meant we had a lot to do, particularly Hannah, who wanted a huge wedding with all the trimmings. My brother was left in charge of the houses, which I knew badly needed proper care and attention. I myself was busy recharging my escorting business, arranging to see Cheryl as well as other regular clients and trying to attract new business through my websites and advertising. I had to make money and fast, not only to start saving and investing again, but to pay for our dream wedding. I started going back to the union meetings and was happy to see that Innocence was still as beautiful, devastating and annoying as always. She was quick to offer me duo work, but I had promised Hannah I would give up that side of the business, so I politely explained why that was now off-limits.

But if Hannah was sure about what she wanted for her wedding, she seemed less and less sure about our plans for life afterwards. It became clear as the days passed that she didn't want to run the housing business, even once she had retired from her role as full-time wedding planner. Nor, it transpired, did she want me to continue escorting. 'But we've bought a house in Westminster,' I said, befuddled at this change of heart. 'We have a huge mortgage because we have chosen to live in the most central part of London and we have chosen to do that for business reasons. We can't just pull out now.'

'We can do anything we want,' Hannah argued. She told me she wanted to retrain to be a primary school teacher. 'But it's six months before the course starts,' I said to her. 'And the course takes a year, and you keep saying you want to have children in eighteen months and look after them full time, so when is the actual teaching going to happen? This is a time to save money and consolidate what we've got. Once the houses are back in order and we're on a more even track, of course you should do whatever training you want.'

As each day went by more and more chinks in my relationship with Hannah emerged. It seemed to me that she flew off the handle for every tiny reason. In retrospect I think she wanted me to push her away, and she was trying to force me to do that, but I didn't see things so clearly back then. Why would she want me to push her away? Perhaps it was the pressure of keeping my secret from our families, perhaps she was nervous about wanting children, perhaps she didn't see a future for us after all. And perhaps it was easier for her to force me to break up with her rather than her taking responsibility for her feelings. But I really don't know what was going through her mind – she certainly wasn't really sharing her feelings with me.

Hannah went out shopping, a lot, often to buy wildly expensive things that we didn't need and couldn't afford, which I was aware was not mere extravagance, but a sign that she was deeply unhappy. I felt concerned for her, but it seemed I was powerless to do anything except infuriate her and fuel her unhappiness and rage. I tried so hard to talk to her, but she just brushed me off, or my concern became the reason for yet another argument. I was getting sick and tired of fighting all the time, and we would either spend our time together in silence or yelling at each other. I think we both felt a sense that we were drowning. We wanted it to work out, but it wouldn't. Neither of us was brave enough to admit that.

All we did day after day leading up to the wedding was argue and fight and reel from one emotionally fraught conversation to another. We started going to counselling at Relate. But going to counselling was useless for us. 'You two need to split up,' is what we should have been told. 'You're mad. You're both mad. Get the fuck out of here and split up.' But we could hardly expect to have been told that. We did almost split up, twice, before the wedding. At six weeks and two weeks before the big day, we looked at each other and one of us said, 'Let's cancel.' We'd already sent out invitations and booked almost everything but we said, 'Let's face the embarrassment and cut our losses now.'

Only we didn't do anything as sensible as that. What we did was discuss it with our respective parents and friends, who told us each to calm down. Pre-wedding jitters it was put down to. But of course they didn't know the half of it. They didn't know that I was paying for the wedding by continuing to escort, and that this was one of the reasons for our arguments. We agreed, somehow, not to cancel but to go ahead, as if everything would straighten itself out. We loved each other, didn't we? And wasn't that enough to make things work out between us? Weddings are supposed to be stressful, after all. Going ahead with the wedding was about the only thing we did agree on. Things got so bad that being with a client for an hour started to feel like a relief from the madness of Hannah and me. Nor were we, about to be man and wife, sleeping together or even in the same room. Hannah was in our bedroom and I'd taken over the working room. The irony of getting up from separate beds and going to John Lewis to check on the wedding list while on the way to marriage guidance counselling in the weeks before the big day was both bitter and unfunny.

We got married in the summer. It *was* wonderful. I felt overwhelmed by love for Hannah. She walked up the aisle to an amazing love song she'd chosen specially, and there wasn't a dry eye in the church. I wept. It was as if all the stress of the last few weeks and months simply floated away. Suddenly everything became perfect. Hannah looked beautiful and, more importantly, happy. We were surrounded by our friends and families and loved ones. Nothing else seemed to matter. All those feelings, all that joy continued into our honeymoon, which was three fantastic weeks of luxury in the Caribbean.

The moment we returned to London, however, it was as if a switch was flipped. Suddenly, everything returned to mayhem. Hannah wanted nothing to do with the houses, and this was the busiest month of the year in terms of letting properties in Cambridge, when you have to get the houses repaired, cleaned and spruced up ready for the new academic year and students looking to rent together. But it was worse than that – my brother had handed back to her all the files on each house and all the keys, but she now apparently didn't know where they were or didn't want to release them to me. I see what she was doing now was to force the situation, to do something so final that it would lead to a split. But at the time that was incomprehensible to me. I just didn't understand what was happening.

It was embarrassing. I didn't want to tell my family about our problems, but it was hard to hide that something was wrong when I had to ring up my brother to ask about the whereabouts of the files or if he had an extra key. 'Oh,' he'd say, 'the files are with Hannah.'

'Yes,' I'd reply. 'Of course. Only I'm going to be running the houses now and I wondered if you had spare copies of anything.'

'But what's Hannah going to do then?' the conversation would go and so it began to creep out that there was something very wrong between us.

Hannah said she was going to take out a loan so that she could buy a large, state-of-the-art fridge freezer and a new sofa. 'But we've already got a fridge freezer and a sofa,' I said, bewildered. In my view, until you can afford to splurge on luxuries like a new sofa, you sit on a bean bag or a box or the floor, and besides, we didn't need to be that frugal – we had everything we needed. 'It doesn't work,' Hannah said about our existing fridge freezer. 'It works fine,' I said, going to check it. The fridge was indeed cold, the freezer freezing. The entire conversation seemed utter madness to me. 'Well I don't like it,' Hannah screamed before leaving the flat and slamming the door behind her. She was using shopping as a drug to lift her momentarily out of her unhappiness. The hangover was, of course, the credit card bill.

We were arguing about fridge freezers and sofas but

really the arguments were about the lack of trust in our relationship, the lack of respect, lack of love. And it seemed that Hannah had a deep desire to force us apart. I feel deep regret that we didn't talk more, say sorry more, love each other more. But by this stage it was too late.

The last straw for me was when I found out that Hannah had taken out a loan from the bank in order to buy a £6,500 sofa. £6,500!

We didn't have that sort of money to spend on a sofa. We didn't have any money to spend on anything except doing up our houses, which was proving hard and I felt Hannah wasn't helping. When I did get to Cambridge, tracking down keys from the house owners for the ones we manage, which was embarrassing to say the least, and also arranging for the tenants moving out of the ones we own, I spent all day working then got back to London only to find that Hannah had locked me out of the flat. She had put the chain on the door and wouldn't let me in. It was one o'clock in the morning. I was trying to catch six hours' kip before heading back to Cambridge and I had to kick the door in on my own house just to get some sleep. We had descended to a point where madness had become normality in our relationship.

July was our wedding. August was our honeymoon and the return to the chaos of the housing business and the chaos of what our marriage was. September saw the chaos intensifying. In early October we managed one night out and I think both of us knew it was our last night out as a couple. We went, with other friends, to a concert to hear the London Philharmonic Orchestra. It was wonderful to hear music played so beautifully, and for one evening it managed to drown out the alarm bells that were by now deafening me. I felt utterly saddened and bereft.

The next day I contacted a solicitor and finally told my brother everything that had been going on between Hannah and me, though I didn't let him know the fact that I worked in the sex industry. A few days after that, a Saturday, I woke up in the flat's spare room (the escorting room) and realized that the flat was unusually quiet. It was 10 a.m. and Hannah and I *weren't* shouting at each other. It was weird. When I walked into the sitting room I discovered Hannah's brother and sister-in-law packing up not just Hannah's stuff but everything in the flat into boxes to be taken away.

'You can't take the computer,' I said. What else could I say? 'The data in it can't be replaced.' They ignored me.

After that things went from bad to worse. We had been married for a matter of weeks and we were heading for the divorce courts and it had unleashed the worst side of both of us, fighting over money and possessions, details I don't want to elaborate on further publicly.

It was all horrible. I sank into depression as well as great sadness over what was happening. Nothing seemed to be working out for me, and all I could see was months and months of financial wrangling with no guarantee that I'd be financially solvent at the end of it. I was extremely worried about money. I had a large mortgage and I was informed by my solicitor that I couldn't escort while Hannah and I were still married because that could be counted as adultery by her and her lawyers. Nor could I move tenants into our large flat to help with the bills because she could then accuse me of either living with another woman or of being gay if the tenant was a man. Such tactics are usually employed during divorce proceedings, but at the time it felt like a stark reminder of how resourceful Hannah was, which ironically had been one of the reasons I'd fallen in love with her.

The thing that made me saddest of all was that Hannah cut off all contact with me and would only communicate through her solicitor. It meant we couldn't discuss what had gone wrong or exactly why she had so silently moved out one Saturday morning without ever discussing her plans. Had she always known? Known at the wedding and on honeymoon? She must have.

When friends ask me what my explanation is, I tell them truthfully that I've no idea. It's awful not to know why someone has left you. You know they are gone, but it seems impossible to accept. All I know is that it amazes me how two people who have been in love and professed love in public can become enemies so fast. I feel embarrassed and sad and ashamed about that. I feel a sense of loss on every level, and I still miss her.

Ten weeks after our wedding, soon after Hannah had left, our wedding gifts arrived from John Lewis, where we had registered our wedding list. When a friend of ours saw the piles of boxes stacked up in the sitting room he remarked that it was the only time he'd ever heard of wrapping paper on the wedding presents lasting longer than the marriage. And of course we even fought over the gifts. We fought over the cutlery her nan had given us and the cushion covers mine had.

In the end Hannah did an eleventh-hour back-down and we got divorced without going to court. And so I kept the London house and ended up paying Hannah's legal fees. The rest of my life was in tatters after all and I was sinking deeper into depression. Money, which for so long had made me high, given me kicks and bought me freedom, now seemed like the least important thing in the world compared to the turmoil I was feeling in every cell of my being. Was it, I began to ask myself for the first time, really worth it?

CHAPTER 12

Secrets Produce Stress

Christmas 2004 was a seriously low point for me. I was grieving for my failed marriage, added to which I was deeply confused about why my marriage had failed. The truth I now realize is that Hannah and I should never have wed, and certainly not under such circumstances – both of us adrift from our 'normal' lives, from our families and friends and what our daily life consisted of. It must have been difficult for her, I imagine, not being able to tell anyone what her husband really did. We found in each other a safe mooring place and clung desperately on to it. And there we did both find love, or at least I know I did. I loved Hannah. I think I always will. But the problem was we also punished each other for the same reason: for being each other's only safe place. It was too much responsibility to carry for each other and so we reacted against it by hurting each other. But it was hard for me to have any kind of coherent thoughts or to be able to explain things to myself, let alone my friends and family, when our marriage ended and I found myself alone, depressed and isolated.

At one point, soon after Christmas, I was in Curry's buying a computer (Hannah had eventually taken the one from the flat with her) when the love song from our wedding came on over the shop's sound system. It was like a tidal wave hitting me, hearing that, the very song and the very version Hannah had walked up the aisle to in her white dress as my bride. I had to hold on to a washing machine, trying not to pass out. Then I managed to stagger out of the shop so I could sit down in the car park long enough to start breathing more normally and not feel that as well as dying inside I was also suffocating and choking on grief.

New Year wasn't much better. That's the thing about depression: it's self-perpetuating, isn't it? You feel terrible, so you don't see anyone and you feel even more terrible. My self-esteem plummeted lower and lower by the day. I couldn't work because I couldn't imagine anyone wanting to spend any time with me, never mind paying me for my company. Nor could I imagine having sex with anyone ever again. If I tried to get an erection I discovered that I couldn't. I felt ugly. It was as if that side of me had just given up, or worse, died. Instead I stayed at home by myself watching the dreadful and distressing images of the devastation the tsunami had caused in south-east Asia.

And because I withdrew so much from both my work and my family life and my friendships – always so important to me – my phone stopped ringing. Friends and family, after all, tried to see me and keep in touch and to help, but if you push them away then that's what happens: you literally push them out of reach.

It took months until something happened to break my cycle of abject depression. Innocence called me and because I didn't recognize the number on my mobile (escorts often have multiple phones), I picked it up to answer it. She wanted to know: a) why I hadn't been to a union meeting in six months, and b) was I free to do a duo with her later that night: an easy, not too demanding job, just me and her with one of her regular clients, a 'lovely couple' and fabulous tippers to boot.

'The guy will be just watching, so there's no danger of any funny business,' Innocence said. 'It would be lovely to see you, darling,' she added flirtatiously. 'I know you're married and I'm sure blissfully happy and not doing duos any more, but it might be worth making an exception for this job. For me. I miss you.' Once, to hear Innocence talking like this to me would have made my blood race. I would have seized the job and been genuinely excited at the prospect of working with her. When we'd done a duo together in the past we'd sometimes taken the party home and continued drinking champagne and having fantastic sex on our own terms and in our own privacy. I loved having

Innocence's long skinny legs wrapped round me and being inside her tight pussy that had a pulsating life of its own.

But even Innocence couldn't cheer me up this time. 'I can't do a duo, Innocence,' I said into the phone. 'Not because I'm married, but because I'm *not* married, not any more. Hannah and I are divorcing.' When she heard this I could hear how surprised she was. Why wouldn't she be? She'd known us for years. Who else gets married in July and is on the way to divorce by the New Year? She continued trying to persuade me to work with her that night.

'Trust me,' I said, 'you wouldn't want to do a duo with me right now.'

Innocence didn't give up. She told me it would do me good to get out of the house and throw myself back into work. Plus, she said, we'd have fun. That made me laugh, a joyless, rueful laugh. 'OK,' Innocence said. 'I can't force you. But you do have to come to the next meeting. I'm not letting you disappear, Andrew.'

I could hear the determination in her voice.

About an hour later – not even that – my doorbell rang, and kept ringing even when I ignored it. I wasn't expecting anyone or anything, but in the end it was curiosity that got me out of bed. It was Innocence. She marched in before I could stop her. I could see her looking at me and looking at the flat, taking it all in: the fact that I wasn't dressed or shaved; the fact that the place was almost entirely empty, save for a vastly overpriced leather sofa, and had the atmosphere of a ghost house. Seeing her witness me at my lowest ebb was almost more than I could bear. I knew that if I tried to say anything, the only sound that would come out would be me choking on my tears.

She didn't ask me any questions, however. 'It's OK,' she said gently. Her voice was a million miles away from the strident tones she uses in the union meetings or the teasing voice she uses with clients. 'I understand. Come on. Come with me.' She took my hand, led me to the bathroom and put me in the shower, washing me down, then drying me like a baby. Then she led me to the bedroom, the very room that was supposed to have been a sanctuary for Hannah and me in our married life. I had not slept in this bed since Hannah left, and hadn't been sleeping in it much even after we returned from honeymoon. As Innocence began to undress, I was finally able to find my voice. 'I don't think I can do this,' I said to her. 'It's not that I don't want to. But I haven't been able to...' I trailed off.

'Shh,' she said. 'It doesn't matter. You'll be fine. You're with me now. Nothing matters. All you have to do is relax and let go. Let go.'

When she had finished undressing, she laid me gently on the bed and began touching and caressing me slowly. This was unlike any sex I'd ever had with her, either for work or for pleasure. This was tender and intimate and, more than anything else, friendly. It wasn't frenzied or passionate. Instead, as Innocence climbed on top of me and put me inside her (to my pleasant surprise an erection had returned) it felt healing. As she moved on top of me, I felt my mental block about sex begin to melt away.

I felt a release, as well as relief. It was as if I could feel electricity coming back into my body, my blood coming back into my veins. I was waking up for the first time in a very long time, and all of these feelings produced the tears that I had been holding in for so long. I cried and cried as Innocence led me to climax, but when we were finished and lying side by side I began to laugh – not loudly, but not joylessly either, and mostly I was laughing at myself and the absurdity of my situation. My marriage had failed. That was my failure, and I had to face that. And yet here I was, stuck in the moment, too depressed to get up or contemplate work; and a few hours away by aeroplane innocent people had lost everything – a great, great many of them their lives – because of a freak of nature. I had to pull myself together and, whatever I might be feeling inside, get back out into the world.

One of the most valuable lessons I learnt from the sad story of Hannah and me was that I could no longer hide my secret from the people I loved most. It was, I had discovered, no way to live. If I was going to continue to be an escort, and I had decided that I would, then I had to face up to that fact, own my decisions and choices and present them carefully to my family and close friends. I was just too tired to continue to live a lie for the sake of propriety. I felt no guilt in my profession, but then guilt is for the guilty. Obviously, I didn't want to advertise my job to all and sundry – dealing with people's reactions and negative energy is both time-wasting and energy-sucking – but time had come to tell my mother and brother and several close friends about my life – my whole life.

The first person I told was my closest childhood friend, Mark. He and his wife Deborah had tried counselling Hannah and me when our marriage was breaking up, but that was an impossible task because it was quite clear there was an elephant in the room that Hannah and I were skirting round. When I went home for Christmas and saw Mark with Deborah and their children, also visiting his family for the holidays, he sat me down and said: 'Look, I know you've got a secret and I know that it contributed to the reason you and Hannah broke up. I know you've kept it from everyone and you can do that, that's your choice, but you need to know that it is detracting from our relationship, because part of you is a stranger to me.' I had wanted to tell Mark right then and there but I felt paralysed. 'You're right,' I said. 'But if I tell you, it could be the trickle of water that leads to the dam bursting and I don't think I'm ready for that at the moment.'

I didn't see Mark much – but then I hardly saw anyone between Christmas and spring – but the day after Innocence's visit, when I felt a dam *had* burst inside me, I went to visit Mark at his house in a quiet suburb of London. It was a long tube journey for me that day, from my empty escorting flat to Mark's back garden with its Wendy house and climbing frame for the kids. Mark and I had been at kindergarten together. We've been through so much of our lives together, only unlike me he has remained a Christian, is married to an equally committed Christian called Deborah and has a respectable job as a senior accountant. Although we have taken different paths in our adult lives, we are still great friends and still love and trust each other. I am godfather to his daughters and I would do anything to protect any of his five children.

It was a warm spring evening when I arrived at Mark's house and we strolled into his garden. I didn't waste much time. I owed it to him to be as straightforward as possible. 'Mark,' I said. 'Do you know what an escort is? Do you know what they do, exactly?' He said he did. He said he knew it wasn't just about taking lonely women out to dinner. Escorts sell sex, he said. I nodded. 'That's what I do,' I continued. 'I am an escort.'

Mark developed into a natural leader early on in his life, and he has always been good in a crisis. His reaction to my news was befitting of his character: it was one of quiet shock, carefully measured. He didn't fall off his chair in surprise but nor did he pretend to be blasé about what I'd just told him. 'Well,' he remarked once he'd taken in what I'd said. 'That's a surprise, but I'm glad you've told me. I'm glad to know. And the fact is we love each other – this doesn't change that at all.' He then paused and thought for a moment. 'Still though,' he added. 'I don't think I'll tell Deborah right now.' We talked for a long time that day. After all, we had eight years of gaps to fill in. I told him about Hannah, and again, being able to talk about the truth was cathartic. We also agreed that the next person I had to tell, however difficult this might be, was my mother.

Some time later I went to see my mum in Cornwall but I didn't tell her to her face. It came out later on the phone. While I was at my mum's, Innocence called me up. She had done a weekend job at some fancy Cornish country-house hotel. It was Sunday night and she wondered if we could travel back to London together. She could do with the company, she said. Since April and Innocence's healing visit, I had begun to start working again, reconnecting with my regular clients and reinstating a couple of my websites, as well as running one or two print ads.

I hadn't done a duo with Innocence or anything particularly hard-core, but at least I was earning money again, and I was glad that regulars such as Cheryl hadn't moved on to new pastures. Or if they had, they were still glad enough to see me back to renew their weekly appointments. Caterina came by for a couple of sessions, though these she said were to be her last. She felt sexually more confident now, she told me, and wanted to try 'going it alone' to see if she could find a boyfriend rather than paying someone for sex.

I was glad to show Innocence something of my home life and glad, too, to introduce one of my London friends to my family. I picked her up on Sunday afternoon and brought her home where we all had a cream tea together, before we set off on the long drive back to London. The next night I decided that things had gone far enough. I had to tell my mother, and I had to do it now, even if that meant doing it over the telephone rather than in person. I called her up and we started to chat. She as always had a lot to tell me about, and then I had told her, by way of introducing the subject, that I had a good friend who was a well-paid stripper, and I'd been roped into helping out in her union. I thought it was the more acceptable end of sex work to start mentioning.

'You'll never meet a nice girl if you hang around with those sorts of people,' was my mum's response.

'The thing is, Mum,' I replied. 'I am one of those people.'

'What do you mean, dear?' she said, in all naivety.

'Do you know what an escort is, Mum?' I asked. She said she didn't really. 'It's a high-class call girl,' I said. 'To put it bluntly. And that's what I am, like a gigolo. Sort of. Like in that film with Richard Gere. Sort of. That's what Innocence is too. We're escorts.'

'Oh,' Mum said. What else could she say? 'Oh,' she said

221

again. Then she rallied. 'Well, you know that I love you,' she said. 'And whatever you do I'll always love you. I have to admit I would prefer you didn't do what you say you do, but I'm glad you have told me.'

We didn't talk about it much after that. It's one thing to tell your mum about being an escort, but that doesn't mean that all the nitty gritty has to be gone into straight off. I asked her not to tell my father – I just didn't feel ready for that – and she said she wouldn't right away, but if I didn't tell him pretty soon then she would because she couldn't keep secrets from him and that was the end of that. She did tell him, too, and, like her, he accepted it. *He doesn't like it*, but he accepted it, accepted me and accepted my choices. What more can you ask for from a parent?

The thing was, I had been worried about telling my parents for so long – or cared that they would find out through something like blackmail – that when I finally told them the truth, it was a bit of an anticlimax. There was no drama, no throwing about of chairs or wailing or gnashing of teeth. It took me a couple of days to get my head around their reaction: I had told them and the world hadn't fallen in, they still accepted me, still loved me unconditionally, and it was this unbelievable sense of relief. Finally, I could be truthful to them, they now knew everything about me, and the result was I felt so much closer to them.

It was true, what I'd said to Mark: that if I told him my secret it would be like the beginning of a dam bursting. It took a while, but in time, I had a frank conversation with my brother and soon after that with my oldest female friend, Catherine, who had been doing some detective work of her own. Mostly people were relieved to know that I was OK. They knew something was going on and, actually, finding out that your best mate or brother is an escort, rather than a drug dealer or pimp or thief, makes for relatively cheering news. Mostly people wanted to know how I was. 'Are you OK?' would be the first question. As in, are you sure you're not psychologically scarred? Once they knew that I was OK, then generally they were OK with it and that's as much as I could ask for.

And so I began to recover. I also began to change in many ways. I cared less about earning money, for example, or rather about earning as much of it as possible. I redefined my boundaries again and took on fewer jobs and allowed myself more time for the things I realized I cared passionately about.

I redoubled my efforts to work with Tender Loving Care and I reconnected with old friends I had lost touch with, whether because of my busy escorting life or my long stint abroad, my marriage, divorce and depression. One of the most important reconnections was with Antiquity Woman. For a few years Antiquity Woman had left both her Cambridge and London homes and had moved into her sugar boy Anthony's huge south London flat. It seemed amazing to me that she would want to do this, but she did, and all I can hope is that it made her feel happy and loved in what turned out to be the last years of her life.

When I saw Antiquity Woman again after my 'year away', it was in hospital. She had suffered a brain haemorrhage and was too ill to return home. I began to visit her every other day and I found it odd that the huge numbers of friends she had always talked about, and who had always enjoyed being entertained at her houses and at her expense, revelling in her civilized and non-judgemental company when she was fit and well, somehow did not manage to find much time to spend by her bedside now that she was so very sick. And she was very sick. Anthony was brilliant and did everything he could and should to help her with this last chapter and the ending of her life. I would come to visit, to find Anthony brushing her hair, or making sure that she was comfortable in her bed. He was always grateful for my coming to see Antiquity Woman as it gave him a break, even if it was just a cup of coffee or a walk to clear his head.

It was always shocking to see Antiquity Woman so frail and ill, such a contrast to the energetic lover of life she once had been. Sometimes we managed to have a halting conversation, at other times I only held her hand, or read to her funny things out of the paper. There was no doubt that she was slipping away, and I knew that time was near when I arrived at the hospital one day to find her having the last rites read by a priest. She died the next day.

It was left to Anthony to organize her funeral, which took place at a private church in a famous quintessentially English village. I did the reading. It was, you could say, a truly society funeral: all kinds of society, that is. It was very fitting for a woman like Antiquity who was born into the privileged life of the upper classes but didn't have a snobbish bone in her body. Lucky her, I thought at the funeral, for breaking out of the rank she was born into. Because it seemed that it was only my fellow escorts and I and her family who were upset by her death and funeral. Many others in their pearls, with clipped and coded ways of talking, seemed curiously unmoved. But, on the other hand, I've learnt that most things are not quite as they appear.

I'm glad I've got to know some of my clients well enough to be by their side at the most intimate moments – in Antiquity's case, hours before her death. But this is unusual. Most of my clients come and go. Some I get to know better than others and some I see once and never again. And then there are some I see repeatedly but never, ever get to know at all. I call these people 'the strangers'. One of them was a woman who came to see me every Tuesday around this time for about six months. I'd say she was in her early forties. She was nice looking and perfectly well dressed but nothing about her was particularly distinctive.

When she first introduced herself over the telephone to make an appointment she said, 'Just call me Sarah.' So I don't even know her real name. She made it clear from the beginning that she wasn't interested in small talk, or a drink or a cup of coffee before or after a session. 'I'd quite like to arrive and simply get to it,' she said the first time. 'I'll always be ready so I don't need warming up or politeness. I'm after straight sex for as long as it happens to last. Don't feel you have to prolong anything just for the sake of anything, and neither will I. That's why I am paying you: so we can keep things very simple and clean and easy and not have to dance around each other. Is that OK with you?' That was the longest conversation, by far, that we ever had.

Every Tuesday afternoon she arrived, left a brown envelope on the sideboard, commented on the weather, waited to be shown into the bedroom and then took off her clothes and waited for me. She liked the radio on while we had sex, but didn't particularly mind which station, and though she was distant and closed off, she responded warmly when I was inside her. I wouldn't go so far as to say we would kiss passionately, but she often, as far as I could tell, reached a satisfying orgasm. When we finished she dressed quickly, used the bathroom briefly, bid me goodbye and was gone. To me she seemed utterly mysterious, but then I am the first to admit that though I love women, I will never wholly understand them.

One Tuesday in the autumn months, almost exactly a year after Hannah left the flat and disappeared so suddenly from my life, the stranger and I were having our regular session when the love song from Hannah's and my wedding came on the radio. The last twelve months passed in front of my eyes when I heard the opening words of that song. Hannah in her dress coming up the aisle, Hannah and I on our blissful honeymoon, the nightmare that our relationship became the minute we touched down on English soil, the days and nights of torment, Hannah leaving, the battle through our solicitors, me collapsing in the car park at Curry's.

I probably stopped for no more than a moment as I experienced this rush of memories. And then I continued with my work. I remember thinking: I'm doing a job to the song my wife came down the aisle to. Then I thought, as I continued working: what a long song it is. Too long for a wedding march probably, but did the bridegroom notice this on his wedding day? No, the bridegroom was too much in love to notice anything except his bride making her way to his side. Then I thought, is this how far I have fallen from such great wonder and love? That here I am listening to this song and I am almost able to regard it as just a song I'm doing a job to. And then I thought: Maybe I have fallen, but maybe, also, this shows that I've finally picked myself up. And then I had one last thought before my client reached orgasm and I was relieved of my duties and that thought was: I'm OK now. I'm OK, yes, but I still miss her.

Sometimes you make an effort and it feels like you are pushing a large snowball up a hill. You wonder what the point of it all is. Of course you have to keep plodding on, but it doesn't always feel like light work. And then every so often, or not very often at all, or even just once, you get the money job. You hit the jackpot. Everything comes good all at once and you think to yourself: I've got the best job in the world. High-class escorting isn't as glamorous a job as it is sometimes made out to be. Clients don't tend to look like Lauren Hutton in *American Gigolo*. Not everyone scores a Billy Piper or a Julia Roberts. But then it happens. You get the call-up. Not very often but always out of the blue.

I got the call-up by one of the agencies I had re-registered with. This time I had been spotted on their website and specifically asked for. It was 10 a.m. when I got the phone call for the job, which generally meant it was someone who had just landed off a transatlantic red-eye flight, checked into their hotel and wanted some fun before getting some sleep or hitting the town. 'The job is imme-diate. It's for you and a female,' the agency told me. 'You need to be boyfriend and girlfriend, and you are seeing a couple at the Sanderson Hotel. On your way please. Now.' Then I was given the room number.

I called Innocence. Ever the pro, she was up for the job. We met just round the corner from the Sanderson and sauntered in and made our way up to the room. A woman answered the door, only she wasn't just any woman. She was someone I knew well, or at least knew well from the television and her albums, which have been huge, international hits. The woman who answered the door, and who was about to pay me to have sex with her, was a major star and unbelievably beautiful. Had we got the wrong room? Was I dreaming? Could things get any better?

The pop star – and I've never told anyone her name – was with her manager, who behaved as if he was a boyfriend too, though she certainly was usually photographed with another guy as her boyfriend – at one point she took a phone call from him and didn't hide the fact that she was having 'extra fun'. Who knows what the real situation was between any of them. All I know is what happened that day. Madam Pop Star, after handing us an envelope full of cash, told us that she and her manager (she called him by his name) didn't want an orgy or group sex. Instead Innocence would take care of the manager/boyfriend figure while I was coupled up with Madam Pop. Oh, poor me. If you've ever stayed in the Sanderson then you will know it is a modern, highly conceived boutique hotel that likes to think it has taken design to another level.

The lift is like standing in space surrounded by the universe with the stars lit up. Walking through the corridors, painted in their dark, metallic colours, is like passing through a tunnel in a laser quest adventure. Beds are often planted in the middle of large, white rooms and there are screen-like walls and partitions in the bedroom so that while it looks very open-plan, you can find private spaces, if, for example, you happen to call up a couple of escorts and you don't want your partner witnessing you having too good a time.

Madam Pop Star was wearing a flesh-coloured silk negligee embroidered with Japanese-style butterflies and chrysanthemums. She was perfectly made up, though it didn't look like she was wearing make up at all. It looked as if her skin had been airbrushed. It was clear she wasn't wearing any knickers. Her eyes were glinting and wide. She was glowing, clearly high on champagne, excitement and anticipation. Part of me could not believe my luck. Another part of me was going: oh shit. I cannot screw up this job. It seemed that the pop star was turned on by me – not so much by me myself I don't think, but by the fantasy she had just made into a reality: calling up an escort and having him do whatever in the world she wants. No fawning. No strings. No pressure. No phone calls. No neediness. No complications. Just sex.

The first thing we did was drink champagne. Then Innocence began seducing the manager while I began caressing the pop star. Slowly, watching me all the time, she took off her slip. Her skin was an even nut-brown all over. Her body was perfect. It was quite a turn on. We began to touch each other but she soon led me over to a part of the room where we could be more private, behind one of the partition walls. There were piles of clothes strewn about, dresses everywhere, which somehow added to the decadent feeling of the hotel room. I got the feeling that she didn't want the manager to share in her good time. Then she knelt down and took my cock in her mouth. It was a beautiful blow job. It was as if she hadn't had sex for a long time and really hungered for it. It felt like she wanted a cock in her mouth, and for a guy, trust me, that feels good. That feels great.

Once she has sucked me for a while, she leads me to the floor which has a large mirror in front of it. It's clear that she likes to watch herself, and as I'm pretty narcissistic, I do too. We have sex in various different positions. It's like she wants everything, all at once. After I've fucked her for a bit, and she has come, she slips away from me, takes off my condom and puts my cock in her mouth and sucks me until I come in her mouth. There is something dirty about her and I mean that in a good, sexy way. She's voracious.

I worry about coming when I know our session is not yet over, but I realize that I needn't. I am hard again in moments as she kneels on all fours waiting for me. I fuck her again, at her instructions. She wants to be fucked hard and fast. 'Fuck me like an animal,' she says over and over again. We both reach orgasm in a frenzy of sweat and groans, then collapse on the bed, tangled in each other and the Sanderson's best linen sheets. Innocence, mean-while, seems to have done a fantastic job with the manager. As far as I can tell they have made their way into the bathroom to fuck in the shower. While they are in there I give the pop star my card – my private business card, not my agency's; usually I would never cut out an agency but this is a special occasion – but I don't say anything and neither does she. We just smile at each other as Innocence emerges from the bathroom and I begin to gather my things, because clearly it's time to go.

As soon as Innocence and I are out of the door, barely able to speak we are so full of what has just gone on, I turn my phone on. There's a text message from a client and I have to call her back. Even though I'm so satiated by my experience with the pop star and all I want to do is collapse at home and relive the morning's events, business is busi-ness, and I'm just about to call her back when my phone rings. The number is unavailable on my screen. It is the pop star. She wants more, she says, as soon as possible. Only this time we'll be alone. I bid goodbye to Innocence and head back to the crazy spacey lifts of the Sanderson.

The pop star wants more. The manager has disap-peared. She is naked this time when she opens the door and pulls me in. There is music on loudly and I realize that it is her new album playing. I feel like I'm almost floating, I'm in a world of such illusion. Who is this woman I'm about to fuck? Who am I to her? Who is the manager, who is the boyfriend? What real relationships does she have? Who can she be properly intimate and loving with? Anyone? My impression is that she has no one for that. That's why she's so hungry for sex with me. That's why she's turned me into a kind of sex god to meet her fantasies and her needs. To satisfy her in this crazy world she has created or that has been created around her. Part of me feels sorry for her, because I can feel her relief – it's palpable – that the manager has left her in peace for a few hours. Far from being her lover, it seems that Madam Pop Star has grown to hate her manager and the constraints that he imposes on her. Imagine being so closely involved with someone who makes your skin crawl. Imagine being desired by so many millions of people but getting proper sexual attention from no one.

She asks me if I like the music. I tell her I love it. She asks me if I have more condoms and lube. I say I have both. She gives me a wicked look and leads me to the bed, turning the music up on the way. She wants anal sex, she says. I almost burst out laughing. She pays me a second time, another envelope, thick with cash. I'm being paid to have anal sex with a goddess. I experience exquisite feelings as I enter her. Penetrating her feels like silk heaven. She touches herself while I move inside her, and I fuck her until we both come.

When we are done, she asks me what I'm doing later. She tells me she has a party to get ready for now, but that maybe I could come back and see her later or the next day. She talks about an awards ceremony she has to go to. She talks about her music and tells me how much she loves her record and don't I love it too. She doesn't ask me a single question about myself, and that's fine. But it's also a wake-up. I can't be on call for her later and tomorrow. I have to look after my bread-and-butter business. I can't simply abandon my life to play sex god to a famous sex goddess who sees me as a sex object. I provide a service for Madam Pop Star and her talk, only of herself, reminds me of that. Her world is not my world, or is it?

CHAPTER 13 ————————————————

Straight Talking

Let's get this straight: I do gay for pay. It's a fact of life that most people who pay for sex are male, so it's inevitable that you're going to get interest from men, and take some on as clients. Any male escort who says that he only accepts bookings from women is almost certainly lying.

I do have boundaries though, much stricter than those I impose on my female clients. No kissing. No penetrative sex. They can watch me masturbate, and – very rarely – there may be oral sex involved, though always with a condom. However, I have to balance these boundaries with the suggestion that there might be something more, if they play their cards right. It's a delicate game, but most of my clients get a thrill from the thought that they will be able to elicit a little more from me. But that is just part of the fantasy that I sell. Coming from a sex worker, it may sound strange, but, in reality, with my male clients, there's actually not that much sex involved.

Let's face it: if you're a guy looking to have sex with another guy, it's not that difficult to secure the services of a gay male escort. There are countless ads online and at the back of magazines. But a straight male escort is quite a rare thing – desirable because he's unobtainable so that it becomes much more of a chase (however artificial), and sex isn't necessarily guaranteed.

With many of my male clients I often feel I'm fulfilling a fantasy they've had since their schooldays. I think most people have had a similar experience, whether male or female, gay or straight. Think back to the time when you're an adolescent, slightly gawky, unsure of your place in the world, and then there's that one person – the captain of the football team, or the most popular girl in the school – towards whom you nurse a secret crush. They walk down the school corridors, good-looking, liked by all, emanating an aura of confidence and charm. You have a crush on them but you want to be a bit like them too. And – most sweetly frustrating of all – you know that never, not in a million years, could you ever be with someone like that.

Just to be clear, I'm not saying that the guys who come to me for my services harbour secret desires to have sex with teenage boys. It's more that they want to be taken back to their youth, to a time of possibility and where sex took place more in the mind than in the body, when sex was naughty, taboo – and we all know how much people like breaking taboos! But as few people's teenage years are enveloped in a Hollywood golden glow, they want to rewrite the script a little, recast themselves as the person who could have been with that athletic, handsome, boy next door. For them I embody vitality and their past youth. For a while – and for a price – they can be with someone clean-cut and youthful, at once within arms' reach yet so tantalizingly far away.

Because of this cheeky boy-next-door quality I have, and because of my strict conditions, my clients tend to be older guys who want me for companionship and the fantasy of being with a straight guy. They like the frisson that comes from being with someone who's not going to fall into bed with them at the sound of a crisp fifty-pound note. Most of my male clients enjoy the flirty, fun nature of our time together, and because of my conditions, any sexual encounter has the feel of the kind of experience they would have had as a teenager, slightly furtive, and more than a little naughty.

Take Roger for example. He was one of the first male clients I took on, and I still see him now, almost ten years later. In fact, he roars with laughter whenever he thinks about just how naive I was when we first met. I remember it well. He had come to Cambridge from London for business, seen my ad and arranged to meet me in a bar. Roger arrived before me and was sitting at the bar, nursing a glass of wine. He asked me what I wanted, and when I said a beer, he nodded his approval. So far, so good – I was living up to his stereotype of a straight guy. We took our drinks to an empty table and, early on in the conversation I brought the topic round to my terms: no penetrative sex, no kissing. He nodded thoughtfully, then asked 'What about rimming?'

Rimming? None of my female clients had ever asked about rimming and I wasn't entirely sure what Roger meant. I was trying to work it out when Roger burst out laughing – the look of puzzlement on my face was all I needed to convince him that I was in fact the straight, even slightly naive, guy I said I was. No false advertising there.

Roger is, in many ways, an ideal client. When I met him, he was in his early forties, reasonably good-looking with a pleasant, intelligent face. He's the kind of guy who takes care of himself, who dresses conservatively but very well. As a senior executive in a media company, he's not short of money but isn't flashy about it. Although I've never been there, he lives in a house by the Thames and apparently it's beautiful. I imagine it to be a bit like him: cleanly minimalist, elegant and restrained. He told me that he's always been very comfortable with his sexuality, and though most people would guess he's gay, he has few camp mannerisms.

He also has a partner, Adrian, and they've been together now for 28 years. I can tell that they're devoted to each other, even though I've never met Adrian. It's the way Roger talks about him: his love and affection for him is clear, the sort of love and affection that only really comes to couples once they've been together for a long time. They are quite different, however. Roger explained to me that the perfect evening for Adrian involves dinner at home with a few friends or a night in with a bottle of wine and a DVD. Roger enjoys those evenings too, but too many of them and he starts to feel cooped up, claustrophobic. Given the choice, he'd much rather go out on the town and take advantage of the nightlife London has to offer, whereas Adrian just never feels comfortable in places where the music is too loud or the room too packed. Roger is upfront with Adrian about me and there seems to be little jealousy on Adrian's part. All in all I think the situation works well for both of them: Adrian can have his peaceful evenings alone, and Roger can go out and party, with a much younger, attractive man by his side.

Going out with Roger is fun, and it's kind of fun playing a different person for an evening, although he also likes to keep me on my toes! For example, Roger might ask me to show up at a bar where he's met some friends. With a naughty glint in his eye, he'll introduce me as 'the new guy in accounting' and I'll spend the rest of the night hoping no one asks me about double entry bookkeeping, or anything else to do with accounting, because I'd be rumbled in a matter of seconds! Saying that, I really don't think anyone believes Roger when he says that I'm an accountant. They probably suspect I'm Roger's bit on the side, the naughty secret that's kept from Adrian – even though, in fact, Adrian knows all. I'm happy to play along with the deception. After all, it doesn't hurt anyone. I'm sure the friends and colleagues I've met have never guessed the real relationship between Roger and me – perhaps they don't have the imagination to think that someone as attractive, charming and urbane as Roger could ever pay for companionship.

In fact, with Adrian, Roger has all the companionship he needs. What he's paying for is the fantasy he has of me being the athletic, attractive, boy-next-door type, the straight boy who would never be interested in him. He says that he feels younger when he's with me, that my youth and vitality reflects back on him. He tells me he loves me, but we both know it's a false love, that it is in no way comparable to what he has with Adrian. He's in love with the fantasy of me that he's created in his mind. I'm not being dishonest, but just playing a role, the role I'm paid to do.

And I'm fine with that. Roger is very well behaved. He's never once tried to push the boundaries of what I'm prepared to do with him. He pays me well – in cash – and whenever I'm out with him, I know I'm going to meet witty, intelligent and interesting people. And to be honest, Roger's adoration of me is contagious – if I'm having a bad day, feeling a bit tired or rough, Roger's attentions appeal to my narcissism and make me feel like the young, strong and attractive man of his fantasies.

Of course, not all my male clients are as fun or straightforward as Roger. Take Leo, for example. He married at a very early age and when he first became my client, in his mid-forties, his children had all grown up and left home. Sex with his wife had completely dried up. I never quite understood what the situation was there – Leo led me to believe that, although there was still a great deal of affection between them, his wife no longer fancied him and was withholding sex.

For me, though, it was painfully clear Leo was gay and that he was undergoing a mid-life crisis, struggling with his sexuality. I think he knew this – whether consciously or subconsciously – but he couldn't change his life in such a significant way overnight. He had to start with baby steps, which was why he came to me. He hired a straight guy because a gay escort would have been too threatening for him. It would have meant coming clean to himself about his sexuality, facing up to the truth that he was gay. It would take him a long time to get to that point. Which is where I came in. And – at the start, at least – he respected my boundaries.

Leo led a conventional lifestyle. He was relatively wealthy and worked in a position of responsibility for a regulatory body. He lived in a nice house in a nice part of London, and I believe he would be living there still, if it hadn't been for the urge he had to explore the part of his sexuality he had concealed for so long.

Leo saw me as having everything that he wanted. I was young, financially independent, having no children to support, 'free' while he was married, having sex whenever I felt like it – and getting paid for it – while his job was dull and unfulfilling. My lifestyle was, for Leo, exotic and exciting. He idealized everything about me, which did sometimes feel a little cloying.

It didn't take long before Leo told me he loved me. Roger told me that he loved me too, but that was part of the game between us – it was fun, flirty, deliberately silly and unthreatening. But with Leo these words became part of a power struggle between us, and I was always uncomfortable when Leo said these sorts of things to me. Essentially, Leo wanted to control me. For example, he would say that if I let him do something to me that wasn't part of my conditions or go over time, he would give me something – more money, a car, an introduction to someone who could help me in my property dealings – but these promises never came to pass. He continually pointed out similarities between us, that neither of us was gay, but here we were, and wasn't that interesting? It was as if he wanted me to say, 'well, actually, I think I may be gay', which would lead him to come out and then we'd sail off into the sunset together.

That was never going to happen. And I was becoming increasingly annoyed with Leo's refusal to treat my boundaries with respect. It was becoming more and more irritating for both of us – I was constantly saying 'No, Leo, you know I don't do that' and Leo was constantly rewording his requests in the hope that I would back down and agree to whatever it was he wanted to try out.

After one particularly trying session I had to tell him that he either respected my conditions, the ones I had laid out right at the start, or he had to stop calling me. We argued for a bit about it, but I was adamant: it was an ultimatum, but a necessary one. Leo had projected on to me all the things that he wanted for himself but, with an early marriage, children and a dull job, he saw as having been denied him. He wanted me to tell him that I was gay so that he himself could come out. Leo never hired me again, but, perhaps a year after it had all come to a head, Leo called me to say that he had finally left his wife and was moving to Spain to live with his new boyfriend.

Roger saw me as a naughty treat, but for Leo I was a stepping-stone on the path to his coming out. Most of my male clients fall between these two extremes. But there was one client who was to change my life and put into jeopardy everything I had worked for and built up over the years. His name was Tim.

Tim called me in the early summer of 1999, having seen an ad I'd placed in a local paper. We arranged to meet, and I have to say, after he left me a tip four times the cost of the hour, I liked him a whole lot more. I would say Tim was possibly better looking than Roger, but I don't think he was more attractive. He was small and slim, dressed very conservatively in a smart-casual, sweater draped over his shoulders, Home Counties sort of way. But he smoked an awful lot – Lambert and Butler – and his skin had a greyish pallor to it. He told me he was in his early forties, not that I would care, but this was just the smallest of the lies he told me. Later, when it all blew up, I discovered he was much older.

He was a director, I believed then, of his own security business, and certainly seemed to be doing very well for himself by the way that he threw money around. He was married, of course. Children. Not gay at all. If you met him you'd be amazed that he had a whole secret life with me, a man. Being in this business I've developed a pretty finely tuned gaydar. But Tim? I never would have thought he had a gay side. But then Tim wasn't like any other client I've ever met.

For a start, regular for him meant *regular*. I saw Tim twice a week, and he didn't want hourly slots: he liked entire days, or evenings, every week, unless one of us was abroad. This went on for eight years. That's quite a lot of time to spend with someone. Because we were spending so much time together, it became difficult to bring up new topics of conversation. 'Um, not much has happened since Monday, Tim, so I'm not sure what to tell you.' Instead, I would show a keen interest in his business, wife, family, and the things he was interested in, which I am not: music, sound systems, cars, boyish stuff. I don't understand paying £2000 for a flat-screen TV, or shelling out to have the wheels on your car upgraded to alloy.

But here's the thing. It didn't matter if I was interested in sound systems, gadgets or fancy wheels or not. What mattered to me was how generous Tim was. If from day one he wanted regular sessions, that same consistency in no way applied to his approach to money. He almost always tipped, but the amount seemed entirely random – sometimes it was a lot, sometimes it was less and sometimes it was fantastic, but I was never able to work out what it was based on.

Clearly when someone tips and visits an escort frequently the onus is on you to lift your level of service in all areas: you prioritize that special client, you make sure you are available to see them when it suits them, you become more amenable to their fantasies and you don't niggle over time. You make an effort with conversation, make sure they are always comfortable and ensure your house or room is always sparklingly clean when they arrive. But with Tim, these things didn't necessarily lead to a better tip. I might try hard, cancel plans in order to meet him and clearly make a special effort, only to receive no tip at all that day. But then it went the other way too. I could be grumpy, tired and uncommunicative, then find a week's worth of wages bundled into a tip. In the end I gave up trying to work it out.

Tim was after what is called the BFE – the boyfriend experience. The BFE means you become more than an escort to someone, but your position isn't as secure (or as controlled) as being a sugar boy with a sugar daddy or mummy. The BFE involves going on 'dates' to dinner, the cinema or bars. You probably don't get paid by the hour but by the day, or perhaps it ends up being a monthly figure. How do you know what the monthly figure should be? Intuitively, and gradually, over time. With Tim and me it just sort of happened, but I'd estimate I earned about £35,000 a year from my six or so sessions a month. Plus gifts.

Ah, gifts. Gifts are not the holy grail some imagine. The Ferrari doesn't tend to be waiting outside your new mews house wrapped up in a bow after a few good sessions. This isn't the movies, remember. *Pretty Woman* doesn't happen in real life. In fact, to remind me of how utterly useless some presents can be, as I write this I am wearing a pair of electric blue shoes that Tim gave me. They are fake 'football boots' and they cost £275. That's madness. I'd rather have a £5 note that I can use than £275 shoes that aren't even comfortable and couldn't look more ridiculous.

One of the skills you need to learn as an escort is how to wangle it so you get gifts you can return. CDs or DVDs may not cost as much as expensive trainers, but you can easily return them and their absence goes unnoticed. Not so distinctive, wearable stuff. Tim would ask me where the shoes were if I didn't wear them regularly. A DVD is easy – you've lent that to a friend, that's why it isn't around – but the shoes? You're stuck wearing the shoes.

I got cannier, in time, at getting better gifts from Tim. Quite often we'd go shopping together. 'Let's get glasses,' Tim would say. 'They'll be *our* glasses.' And so I'd steer him to John Lewis where he'd buy thin, delicate champagne flutes. Well, nothing thin or delicate lasts long in my kitchen and so once 'we'd' used them together, I'd put them away carefully, then return them, rather than letting them get broken, which is what I would say had happened, a note of sadness in my voice. I did a lot of my Christmas shopping through returning clients' gifts. You can get anything at John Lewis!

Of course, a lot of clients know this is going on and recognize it as part of 'the extras', just as an accountant might charge a client the time it takes to eat his lunch in between doing his books. That doesn't meant you don't have to know when to stop. No one likes being taken for a ride or always being the one seen paying for everything. I learnt quickly that if Tim and I went to a bar then I should offer to buy the drinks. I wasn't *really* offering, of course, but I knew that when I said, 'Let me get the drinks, Tim, what would you like?' he'd reply, 'Oh thanks, but I need to break a note so use this,' and he'd give me fifty quid on the understanding that I'll then use the change to buy us both drinks for the rest of the night.

In those early days, I didn't know how much me making a show of paying for Tim turned him on. He let me know gradually and carefully just how important it was for him, and because it was so gradual and so in keeping with other eccentricities I could never quite get to the bottom of, such as the basis for his tips, I accepted it as just a client's foibles.

Although my sexual boundaries with Tim never changed, it started to get a bit more dodgy on the money side of things. I should have stuck with cash. But of course, hindsight is 20/20, and when Tim asked me if he could start paying me by cheque, despite huge misgivings, I said OK. After all, Tim was, at the time, my most regular client. He certainly gave me the most money and gifts, he was generous in his tips, so I felt obliged to blur the boundaries with him. He told me it was all legit and that my name would appear on the accounts showing everything was above board. The reason it is so easy, he explained, is because his business partner sees a female escort and they've both agreed to give themselves the same 'perk'. And doing it this way means he doesn't have to draw huge amounts of cash out of his personal account, which he shares with his wife.

I wasn't wild about the idea of taking cheques from Tim. Mostly I was concerned about the possibility of a cheque bouncing after my experience with Sonia Blue-chip and her magic post-cashed bouncing cheque trick. Could Tim pull off the same thing? I didn't think so, but I felt I shouldn't be too careful. Plus, I love working with cash. I like all the different aspects of dealing with it, not least receiving it.

Agreeing to accept cheques from Tim was to lead to the most difficult period of my life. I should have trusted my instincts and insisted on cash. But who was to know that I was nurturing something that would eventually implode to such a degree?

CHAPTER 14

The Laying On Of Hands

A year almost to the day after Hannah and I married, I met Jennifer. I met her at the wedding of a childhood friend in Cornwall, mere miles from where Hannah and I had wed. She, a great friend of the bride, was a maid of honour. I was one of the ushers. It was the usual story. A summer weekend in the country, lots of alcohol, anyone single eager to stop being so. I fancied Jennifer as soon as I saw her – most men would. She's petite with fair colouring and really cute feet. In terms of love or anything remotely serious, I simply want a good, true, loving woman. That shines out of a woman and it's that, not the length of a leg or the narrowness of a hip (though she doesn't fall short in either department), that is the real turn-on.

I fancied Jennifer, but what I didn't know was that, even before meeting me, she was already intrigued. A few weeks before the wedding, the bride had had her hen party at my flat. I'd lent her the flat for the weekend for her and her friends to run riot in (I was on a stag weekend in Amsterdam, but that's another story). I hadn't at this time told anyone but Catherine, Matthew and my mother about being an escort, and so the secret was very much still under wraps. The rumour persisted, and still does among most of my friends from home, that I was a pimp. Who is this guy with a huge flat in Westminster who got married and divorced in a year, Jennifer had wanted to know during the hen weekend. By the time the wedding came round she had built me up in her imagination as a risky bad boy, which was exactly the kind of guy she is attracted to. I was, you could say, exactly her type.

Luckily for me, she accepted the real-life version too. Our friends had something of a DIY wedding, with all their mates pitching in to put up the marquee, do the flowers, be the DJ, set out the hired furniture and so on. It was all a lot of fun. Only the night before the wedding, just as a large group of us were about to set off for a local nightclub, an alarm bell went off in my head. The alcohol, brought by mates of the groom back from France in a van, had been dropped off at the marquee that evening. The marquee that we'd put up in the local village football pitch. If I were a young lad on a Friday night, a bit broke and up for a good time, mightn't I and a couple of friends check out the marquee put up in a semi-public place to see if it was a hoarding place for booze? You know what, I just might.

As we got to the marquee, at about one in the morning, I was proved right. Soon after, two cars drove in both filled with groups of boys. How do you, armed with a torch, plus a friend and a couple of girls in high heels, take on two carloads of rowdy, testosterone-fuelled lads in the dark car park of a football pitch basically in the middle of nowhere? I went straight up to the car smiling like a lunatic. What I didn't want was for one of them, or worse all of them, to get out of the car and see how few we were compared to how many they were.

'Hello there,' I said, as if we were meeting in a National Trust car park on a sunny afternoon. 'How you doing? Just on a drive, are you? This is a dead end, though, so I think you may have taken a wrong turning. Easy enough to do. The way *out* is over there.'

They turned tail and left. We went to have a few more drinks, me feeling impressively brave now and I was getting nicely sloshed. Plus, the next thing I know, I've landed the lovely Jennifer. She comes back to my house for a delicious pre-wedding one-night stand. When I drop her off the next morning at the house where the wedding party are getting dolled up I know she's hungover and feels bedraggled, but she still looks devastatingly sexy. Three hours later at the wedding she is transformed into a sleek beauty. Our one-night stand becomes a two-night stand. And then the weekend was over.

Jennifer was keen to meet up again, and in theory so was I. But I was still recovering from the break-up of my marriage, and at this time she represented a risk, being such a close friend of the bride. I was also, after my leave of absence, throwing myself back into work. A two-night romance was one thing, but to start dating a girl like Jennifer, who I wouldn't ever want to deceive, felt wrong. The timing was just impossible. I couldn't handle it. I didn't want to start lying to her, but I couldn't handle getting serious enough with another woman to tell her the truth either, especially a woman connected to my home life. Instead of agreeing to meet her I sent Jennifer an enormous bunch of flowers on her birthday, which she had told me was soon after the wedding, along with a note saying that my job (I didn't go into specifics) made it impossible for us to see each other again.

Well, Jennifer was not having any of that nonsense. 'Oh,' she said when she rang me to thank me for the flowers, 'what you said in your note? I don't see why whatever job you've got should stop us from having fun. If you don't want to hang out, fair enough, but I'm not looking for anything serious if that's what you're worried about.' Basically, she reeled me in by making out that she was happy to have some kind of non-serious, open relationship, when in fact she wasn't. She said that whatever I did for work wasn't her business, but after date three of casually seeing each other – and having a great time I must say – she went on my computer and found documents and emails relating to my escort work.

Jennifer works for a well-known TV company. She's a bright woman trained in investigative research. It didn't take her long to put two and two together. She said she was surprised – she hadn't imagined I was an escort. We'd only been on three dates when she found out and so our relationship would have been easy to break off without too many tears or recriminations. I was furious. How dare she go on to my computer and look at my personal files? This was the type of thing that you'd dump a girlfriend of six months for, not to mention one you'd only known for a few weeks. But when I said that to her, she stood her ground. She told me she knew that I was hiding something from her, and that was the only reason for her looking on my computer. And now she knew what I was hiding, we could be honest with each other.

'Honest?' I spluttered. 'You just looked on my computer, at my private stuff. And not just that, what about my clients, who trusted me to protect their identities?'

She assured me that she had seen no names. And that she didn't care what I did, she just wanted us to hang out together and be comfortable with each other – such a big secret would always come between us. I calmed down as she explained that really, her finding out about what I did was a good thing – and it didn't matter to her what I did – she had grown up in a liberal household. Her dad is part hippy, part boffin who worked in a lab in California for a few years on missiles before moving back to an extremely pleasant suburb of London to continue bringing up his children. While they lived in LA they had a friend who had been an escort, she said. No problem.

The thing is, it was a problem, or it became one. For the first six months or so we both played at keeping our relationship casual, which is usually just the man's cop-out-of-commitment story. But by early 2006 it was clear that we more than enjoyed each other's company. We were falling – had already fallen – for each other. We decided to get serious and 'go exclusive'. I agreed to give up duos. I talked about it perhaps becoming time for me to begin to scale back my escorting business and concentrate on something else. It's just that I wasn't yet sure what that would be, apart from property, or the PhD I'd been meaning to do for ten years.

I have to confess, I found it quite difficult to give up doing duos with Innocence. I didn't want to be with her, and she drove me bananas in the union meetings, but there was no denying it, our 'work' sex all too often drifted into 'real' sex and it was quite clear that we both got more than just work out of it. That would have to stop, but it seemed that I kept delaying the last duo job. It was always a case of me saying to Jennifer, or more often only to myself: just one more for the road.

Which explains why I took the job with Mile High Bob. It wasn't planned, I told myself, wasn't by arrangement, but just sort of happened, when at 8.49 a.m. one crisp morning I received a phone call. At 8.49 in the morning I'm doing what most working people do at ten to nine on a weekday: rushing about, throwing the duvet over the bed, gulping down coffee, putting dirty socks into the laundry, taking a shower, chivvying Jennifer out of the door because soon she will be late for work. But then the phone rings.

'Hello.'

'Andrew. How's it going?' An American accent. But who? It's too early in the morning for me to identify the client by mentally flicking through the voice bank I have archived in my head.

'I'm fine,' I said, my mind still blank. 'How have you been?'

'Great, Andrew,' the voice said. 'I'm in London. Just arrived off a plane from Barbados.'

Ah, Barbados. That means this is Mile High Bob. He's not American at all, but Canadian with a Barbadian lilt in his voice. A fairly complicated client, but one that any male escort sees often enough. Wants enough pseudo-gay action to turn him on, but not a jot over anything that might imply he has inclinations that way himself.

'So when can you get here?' Demanding too.

'In about twenty-two minutes and six seconds. More or less.' Worth it. 'How was the flight?'

'High!'

I felt my brain switching gears. The things I had planned to do today – writing up something for the sex workers' union, fixing something in one of the houses I owned, going out to dinner with my brother, spending the night with Jennifer – these things would have to be postponed. Fast. Not for hours, but days. A job with Mile High Bob inevitably took the whole day and night, and then a whole day after that.

I began frenetically making calls while trying to shave and shower. I told Jennifer I'd drop her at work in a taxi, because something had come up, and I would be passing her office in Upper Regent Street. I didn't tell her what. She knew that it must involve escorting and she didn't want to know any nitty-gritty details. She worked in an office building opposite the Langham Hotel, which is where Mile High Bob often stays, so it made sense for me to drop her off on my way into my own workplace. The Langham has two separate ways in, one for the hotel and one for the restaurant. I needed to find female escorts who were familiar with the hotel layout and weren't going to wander about clumsily. You don't want a succession of young nubile women floating around a hotel all looking for the same room. You want them to go straight from street to lobby to lift to room like an arrow, without having to pause. At this time of the morning, hotel concierges are less amenable to escorts, especially females, who are often more conspicuous than their male counterparts.

But navigating the Langham will be the least of it. Mile High Bob doesn't like to see 'escorts'. He just wants a succession of natural, normal girls – the girl from the reception desk of the hotel, the woman who sold him the necklace for his wife, friends of mine who simply want to party with me and him. Anything that at least appears not for sale and therefore beyond his financial reach. And though his desire is all-consuming, he can't actually do too much. He's too full of coke. That's why I'm the first person he calls. So that I can be him and fuck 'my friends' for him, and he can watch. And it's not just the girls he likes looking at, I've noticed. I've seen his glance lingering on my tanned smooth skin for longer than a completely straight guy should, although I make no sign of noticing this – which is just how I should behave.

Now what I want to say to him is: what the fuck are you expecting? Do you think I would ring up a friend who's not an escort and say, 'Oh hi, it's me, just wondering if you want £500 to come over for an hour and have some sex while a Canadian businessman watches us and gets high on coke?'

Of course I didn't say any of this to Bob. I told him: 'No problem,' and on my way to the hotel started texting all the girls I regularly work with to see if any were free, crossing my fingers that at least one would be and that she would be checking her phone at 9 a.m. My phone never goes unchecked. Already this morning I've dealt with several neurotic texts from Tim. But though Tim is a needy client right now, it is Bob who is my priority and that means finding normally behaved, quickly available escorts who don't look like escorts.

When I got to the hotel, however, I discovered that Bob, unable to contain himself, had already called a girl – Rachel – whom he had chosen from a website. This bought me a little time, though not much, because though Rachel is fabulous-looking, she was still not good enough for Bob, because having called her himself even he can't quite manage to delude himself that she just happened to show up for some fun.

She was already in the shower when I arrived. Bob, jetlagged and still in another time zone, was already snorting cocaine. He offered me a line. Saying no is not in keeping with the spirit of things – we're all friends here after all – but I have to be careful with coke, or any drug, including alcohol, because if I have too much I can't get hard, so I pretended to snort it, and Bob, coasting on the lift of a fresh hit, didn't notice that I'd just amalgamated my line into the second line he'd cut for himself.

Meanwhile my phone pinged and it was a Brazilian escort called Rosa letting me know that she was available, up for a job and to call her back with the details. Rosa is a real pro, who doesn't look like most people's idea of an escort, but who is an utter natural and very successful (it's no coincidence that she checks her phone as regularly as me). I knew she'd instinctively understand the situation, even though I would only be able to explain Bob's requirements hurriedly and in code.

'Rosa?' I used her working name to indicate I was with a client.

'Andrew, how are you this morning?'

'I'm good. Are you at college at the moment, my lovely?' Immediately Rosa knew that she had been cast in the part of an innocent, hard-working student. With a naughty side. 'How is your economics degree?' Let's at least not stray *too* far from the truth. Rosa, after all, is an economics master of sorts. She understands money perfectly, it's just that coming from one of Rio's favelas, growing up surrounded by gang violence, drugs, music, desperation, despair, hope and determination, she is self-taught. Now she owns a house outright in the UK, and has bought a house for her mother in Brazil. But she's been through a lot to get to that place, having been deported twice, once when she was supposed to be grateful for being 'saved from sex trafficking', and twice escaped back to London. She is beautiful, determined, intelligent, forthright and packed full of life's delicious dynamite. As well as the houses, she has bought EU citizenship, paid for an education and tucked away enough money to pay for the education of the children she hopes one day to have.

'I'm out at the moment,' Rosa said to me down the phone. This meant she didn't have any sexy stuff with her. At 9.15 a.m. it was not surprising that she had been caught on the hop. She knew she couldn't ask any direct questions or risk stepping out of the role play, in case Bob was listening carefully to our phone conversation and could hear her voice through the phone. 'Don't worry,' I said airily. 'Bob doesn't mind. He knows you are on your way to college.' The less Rosa looked likes an escort, the better for Bob.

'I'm at the gym,' continued Rosa. This meant she hasn't showered, shaved or put on make-up.

'Bob doesn't mind,' I replied. 'He has a shower in his room and he'll probably want to watch you wash,' I said loudly, to give him a little treat. 'We are quite excited thinking about you,' I added, which meant: can you come over immediately?

Her reply: 'Have you got everything we need?'

Mine: 'Don't worry. It's all sorted.' I.e.: I've got plenty of protection, lube, blindfold, poppers and yes the money is sorted and you will get paid up front as soon as you get here. I'll make sure of that.

Anyway, money is not a problem for Bob. He is a man who swoops into Europe, buys large plots of land and builds educational centres on them. He deals in a lot of cash, and doesn't mind shelling it out for something he wants, but you have to make sure you get a lot of money up front, and that there are reserves in the room because the job goes on for so long and Bob gets into such a state that by the end of a thirty-sex-hour session it's as much as he can do to wave goodbye, never mind get down to the hotel lobby and request a visit to the mother-ship safe where he's stashed his cash reserves. You want that trip done before the party begins and in case he becomes less friendly, especially when I'm the lead person with a female.

Bob had been enjoying what he could hear of our conversation. He had already complained about Rachel, the escort who was now emerging from the shower. He wasn't interested in watching her wash, he said as he chopped another line, but even though she was 'practised and plastic', he did add that 'we can do her for half an hour'. He's more goal orientated than a pastoral person, is our Bob. I, on the other hand, thought Rachel was gorgeous. She was a blonde bombshell with a slim body, perfectly pert breasts and lovely skin. She looked like one of those girls on the front of *FHM* – not my type but fantastic to look at.

I nipped into the loo and flashed a text to Rosa to give her a more accurate lowdown of what she can expect. '22, econ king col, Halloween, party, ;-) , yes K, no A, extension, fine, Italian.' This translates as: you are 22, studying economics at King's College, and we met at a Halloween party. You will need to fake and take cocaine, yes I've already had a line, and there will be kissing but I've got you out of anal. If we play our cards right the job may go well over time, things are OK so far, and remember: you are a student from Italy, not a sex worker from Brazil.

When I came out of the bathroom Rachel was sitting propped up against the pillows on the room's big bed with her legs bent and apart. Her hair was wrapped in a towel and she was wearing a pink swimming costume (Bob must have asked her to come as a beach babe) that revealed the contours of her pussy. I'm a polite well-brought-up Englishman so I didn't ogle her, but I did become turned on. Rachel sensed this and knew that I knew that she knew this, and my response to the subtle change of atmosphere – sexual chemistry has reared its head – is to desperately hope that I will not be a disappointment to her.

Certainly she wasn't to me. She was fantastic, and appeared not to be merely going through the motions. Her pussy was wet, she was kissing my mouth and when I was inside her I could feel her responding to me. I don't know what Bob has asked her to pretend, or what charade he has asked her to play – that we are real lovers? – but that's what it felt like and I decided to go along with whatever happened, and what happened was that, while I was pumping away, she ran her hand down my back, held my bum and stopped me for a moment, as if to say: I like you,

I'm enjoying this but hold it here. Stop for a moment, and let's go slooooower, so that when we began again in a different rhythm, *her rhythm*, and I knew for sure that whatever else was going on this was no show sex, even though a few metres away Bob was naked on the bed, jabbering away to himself and us while playing with his semi-soft cock.

Only here came Bob angling in for a close-up and so though the real sex continued, show sex is all we will let Bob in on – fake moans covering a real quickening of breath – because, sensing his disrespect, she didn't want him to see that she was enjoying herself. It was her way of saying: I don't like you, don't really want you to be any part of this and this is an area I don't want you to be included – and so the strange situation began to occur where she started to fake an orgasm in order to cover her real one.

The fake orgasm is almost always the same. You always know how it goes. It's like the jazz band at a pub who play the same set every Sunday night for the tourists. At 9.30 p.m., on the dot, they stop for a twenty-minute break and at 10.50 p.m., on the dot, the female singer begins singing solo. When that solo finishes, the band is done for the night. You know, when that woman starts singing alone, that's it. No encores, no deviation, over time. It's the same when someone fakes an orgasm. There is the tonal noise stage – here we go, getting there – which morphs into drawn-out moans and climaxes with a high-pitched shriek and finishes with a sigh of relief.

Some female escorts never fake it. An escort I know called Laya never makes any effort to fake anything with a client and if asked by the client if she's enjoyed herself, she says no. And guess what: some clients love that. If I'm doing a duo with someone of course I want them to have all the fun they want, but we're mainly working. In all of this I'm still learning, will never know everything and love the fact that women I'm sure will always be wonderfully mysterious to me.

I like it when women say to me: this is what happens to me and my body and this is what I need to make it happen. Us men want to know. We don't want to do a bad job in sex. We don't want women saying: my God, this is going on for ages. What *is* he doing down there? How can I get him out? Or: why is he banging away at me like that? Can't he tell that it's just not happening? No. Mostly we can't. We need you to say to us: go to the left a bit, or if you can't say it just move us to the right spot or let us know unequivocally when we've hit it. Because from a man's point of view doing unsuccessful oral for an hour results in one thing only and that is lock jaw.

Lecture over. Back to what at least appeared to be successful sex. Because I could actually feel Rachel's pussy walls contracting in ever-increased rhythms around me, so I was pretty sure she was getting close to orgasm, and I certainly knew that I needed to calm down somehow, though without changing the rhythm otherwise I was going to come too quickly and she wouldn't come at all – nor could I afford to lose sight of the fact that I didn't know how long I was going to be here today, that Rosa was already on her way over. I could feel Rachel making things go faster and faster and so I also thought, this is such a lovely morning, and while the fake moans were happening, at the same time Rachel's pussy was getting tighter and tighter and just as she was about to come for real Bob put his face right up close to ours and stage-whispered to me: 'Will you do anal?'

We lost it. The real orgasm disappeared; the fake one quickly dispensed with. I could tell just from a flicker of her eye that it was not what she wanted. Bob started chopping up more lines of coke for us to take – as if that was the answer for everything, which I suppose Bob has decided it is.

'I only do anal with a girlfriend,' I said, which was a ridiculous thing to say and Bob knew it. Chances are I'd be doing it later with another escort, one who has agreed in advance that she's up for it, for the right price. I couldn't think off the top of my head who that would be – I'm not an mobile escort agency after all, no matter what Bob assumes – so I knew I'd probably end up ringing Jonny Bedlam. What mattered now was that Rachel felt safe. I could tell by her expression that she was thanking me. It wasn't pure altruism on my part. Girls cover for me all the time too.

For me the escorts are top of a top-ten list of the most important things in any situation and I don't even know what the other nine are. I will pander, make up stories, throw in fantasies and be as nice as possible to the client, but there's no way I'd allow an escort to be forced to do anything they don't want to do on my account.

Anyway, Bob isn't ever a real problem. He knows the boundaries and he isn't abusive. He's just overenthusiastic and spoilt. He'll get what he wants in time. Rachel was getting dressed. She had that flushed look of the almost orgasm. I knew she'd be going home to finish off with her fingers what we'd begun. I wished I could have joined her. No, I didn't! I had a girlfriend I loved, so of course I didn't. And who gets to leave work just because you find yourself in the mood for getting off? That day, my work was in a suite in the Langham Hotel. I could hear Bob chopping more cocaine on the coffee table. Rosa had just texted me to say she was walking through the lobby and on her way to the room. I sent a quick one back to her and then texted Bedlam to tell him to start sending the cavalry, or, as Bedlam used to put it: *An Anthology of English Pros*. I also told myself that this really will be my last job doing duo work, because if that's what I've promised Jennifer, then that is what I must do. Though not without regret, because right now, I'm really enjoying the work.

It's funny how life intervenes with your intentions and gives you a reminder of where your priorities should lie. Not long after my session with Mile High Bob, I decided I should start to wind down my escorting business. I booked a job with a new female client and wondered how many more women I would meet and see as an escort again. The job is booked for a Sunday evening at 9 p.m., and because I have some time on my hands, I decide to go to church for a 6ish evening service. Holy Trinity Brompton is a happy-clappy church in central London and going there I'm struck by a feeling I have had before, which is: when is this service coming to an end? I'm still pretty anti-church at this point, and I only need to attend a service about once a year to be reminded why I don't go any more. Why does it annoy me so much? It's a thousand things. It reminds me of all the baggage that goes with the church, which I became all too familiar with in my past: the naivety on one side and the politics at work on the other.

I sat at the back so I could get up and leave early and be home in good time to get ready for my nine o'clocker. Thank God I did because the service was indeed neverending. But however much Church, and this particular service and sermon, irritate me, I always enjoy giving the sign of peace – that bit in a service when you shake your neighbour's hand and either say, 'The peace of Our Lord be with you,' or reply, if they've said it to you, 'And also with you.' This time I shook hands with a woman sitting behind me, near to the very back of the church. The woman struck me as we shook hands; I felt some kind of connection with her. Nothing dirty or sexual or presumptuous – just something human and basic and warm. The woman, youngish and serene-looking, had that sort of timeless look about her that you see in well-cast period dramas. I felt like I might have been shaking her hand a hundred years ago.

Just as I think we'll be freed, the Rector announces a baptism. I take this as a sign to leave, and start to quietly exit the church. The period-drama woman, I notice, is also getting up to leave. We smile politely, and give each other that knowing look that says: this service has run over big time, then go our separate ways. I hurry home and just have time for a shower before the doorbell rings with my nine o'clock appointment. It is the woman from the church!

I don't know who was more surprised, her or me. But you know what, you don't get a message much more powerful than that. Once the woman and I had laughed about how small and crazy the world is, and then had gentle sex, I realized for certain that I wanted to be with my woman, not flouncing about doing duos with Innocence. I called Innocence as soon as my client left and told her that I'd still see her in union meetings but that as far as working with her was concerned, or anything else, that was over.

Jennifer was glad that I had closed a part of my escorting life down for her, but she wanted more. If we were going to live an honest, open life together, perhaps get married and have children as we had begun tentatively talking about, then she didn't want to hide what I did from her parents. What? OK, OK, it's true that I've learnt the hard way about hiding crucial facts about yourself from your family and close friends, but telling your girlfriend's dad that you have sex with strangers for money? No matter how 'new age' and accepting he was, surely – as the father of my girlfriend – he'd have a problem with what I did for a living. I really didn't want to tell him; in fact, the thought filled me with dread. But in this Jennifer got her way.

Jennifer had already strategically leaked the information to her mum and her brother and sisters, and they were fine with it. Again, this was overstepping my boundaries – it was *my* secret, *my* life, so I felt that it was *my* prerogative to tell who I want to tell. And since the cat was now out of the bag she thought her dad should know too and she thinks it would be better coming from me. In a couple of weeks we were all going to California together to one of their family's friends' wedding. Ted should know before that, Jennifer said. I agreed with her, but it's just that this was one conversation I did not want to have. Ted, Jennifer's dad, may have long hair, smoke, wear denim and be open-minded, but as well as being a bit of a hippy genius, he's also a father. Jennifer's father. And Jennifer's boyfriend was about to tell him that he's a prostitute. I wondered if there might be a fight.

Jennifer emailed her mum to ask her advice. Would Ted (Jennifer calls her dad by his first name) be OK about Andrew's job, did she think? The email came back: 'I have been with your dad for thirty-five years and I just can't say what his reaction will be.' There was nothing for it but for me to take the plunge. We made a date to go over to their house for a Saturday lunch. It was one of those rare sunny and bright February days when you think everything might just be all right after all. But was it? My nerves were jangling all through lunch, and when it was over, Ted strolled into the sitting room and switched on the football to see what was happening. The rest of the family, I noticed, discreetly wafted away, leaving the two of us alone together.

'Ted,' I began. 'I wonder if I can have a word with you about something.'

'Oh?' he said, seeming to note the seriousness in my tone. 'Are you and Jennifer getting engaged?'

'No, not engaged,' I said. 'Not yet anyway. No this is something else. About my job.' I started to lose my nerve. Ted was still watching the football and we were sitting next to each other on the sofa, which made for an awkward angle for conversation. 'The thing is,' I continued, beginning to mumble, 'I wanted to tell you … I feel like … Mary knows and a few other people and I don't want you to feel left out. It's about my job.'

'Yes,' Ted said, beginning to look puzzled.

'Well, basically. You know my job. I don't like lies. I don't want you to feel left out …'

I kept going round and round. Then I blurted it out. 'I'm an escort.'

Ted was silent for a moment when he heard this. I knew he was taking what I'd said in. I wondered if he was going to blow up, or even hit me. But he didn't do either. In fact, he seemed OK. He went with his non-conformist side and accepted me. He didn't even really want to talk about it much. 'That's OK,' he said. 'As long as Jennifer is OK with it, it doesn't seem like my business much. As long as you are careful and safe, which I'm sure you are. Are you?'

'So safe,' I replied. 'Absolutely. Of course.' My relief must have been palpable. I felt a huge weight lifting off my shoulders. I felt like Jennifer and I could now start the next chapter of our lives together.

I had decided to put my flat on the market a few months earlier – prices never seemed higher back then – and put my furniture and belongings into a cheap storage unit in Cambridge, making sure my Cambridge properties were all operating perfectly, and then planning a retirement party. Yes, retirement. I had finally decided after ten years as an escort, ten glorious, odd, mad, happy, unhappy, chaotic, fun years that I was going to hang up my boots, or rather turn off my phone. Then Jennifer and I would go travelling for a few months (she was by now consulting on a freelance basis for factual TV programmes) before returning to the UK and beginning our new life together. Days after I registered my flat with an estate agent I was offered the (enormous) asking price by a buyer who was not in a chain. My new life, I felt, was about to start. I felt like the sky was the limit.

The sky fell in at 9.30 a.m. on 19 March 2007, a date that will be forever etched in my memory. I wasn't in London that day. I was in the countryside enjoying a day out with one of my godsons. My phone was switched off, something that was happening more and more since I'd begun to scale down my business. When I switched it on there were a number of messages and texts for me, all of which made my blood run cold. One was from a police officer requesting that I call him back with what seemed to me a great deal of urgency, and the other two were from my downstairs neighbour saying that the police had been round to my flat and that she had let them in so they could do a thorough search of the premises.

How can I describe how I felt hearing this? You know what it's like when you swing high on a swing and it feels like your heart hits your stomach? That's how I felt, only not in a good way. Why were the police there? Was it because of my business? And if so, why now? Why not a week, a month, a year earlier?

The first thing I did, after dropping off my godchild, was to call my lawyer friend to get the name of a solicitor. I told her I couldn't talk or explain right now, but that I needed help. She understood immediately and told me that any time I needed her she was at the end of the phone. Then she gave me the name and number of a solicitor, whom I called. He told me to sit tight and not to call the police officer back, that it was better if he did that, and

273

that he'd ring me as soon as he could to tell me what all this was about.

He rang back quickly. The police, he explained, wanted to talk to me very seriously about a theft of £48,000. Not only that but about the 'money laundering' I had been doing on behalf of my client Tim, who was now under arrest. Suddenly, things clicked into place. Tim's increasingly erratic behaviour of late (I thought it was a midlife crisis) and obsessive texting made more sense.

I should explain things a bit more, things that hadn't seemed hugely important to me at the time they were happening because they just seemed like part of Tim's quirkiness when it came to 'our relationship'. After all, he had been one of my longest-standing and best-paying clients. He was also married, supposedly straight, a father and a successful businessman. Anything he did with me is part of his secret, mysterious life. By definition, that is going to be mysterious and complicated and not totally explainable. I am used to that. You see things as an escort – people's desires and fantasies – that aren't allowed to be aired in everyday life. Foibles and odd requests stop surprising you. Certainly they did me. And Tim's weren't even that odd, compared to some.

As I've said, what Tim wanted was the BFE, the boyfriend experience. His fantasy involved wanting the *appearance* of being on equal terms with me. He didn't want me clock watching, for example. He wanted to go out for drinks and dinner. He wanted to talk and hang out, and though he would have run a million miles from sex (which would have broken his fantasy of being with a straight guy), he wanted us to have a sexy-ish flirtatious time together. What he didn't want was for him always to be reminded that he was the client and I was the escort. Tim never stinted on paying me, and if the amounts were random – they had been right from our very first encounter – they were always higher than my bottom-line hourly rate. So if he wanted to give me cash at the beginning of the evening or before a shopping trip so that I would then pay for stuff, that was fine by me.

I've already described how he went from paying me by cash to paying me by cheque, as well as the cash he gave me for expenses while we were out together. But after a few years he told me that he wanted to be paid too, as part of his fantasy of our roles being fluid and reversible. What happened is that he would give me some money and then I would pretend to be the client. It was slightly odd but by this point we had seen each other for six years and there was a level of trust between us. And all this would have been fine, except for the crucial fact that the money he was using turned out not to be his, and the money that I was paying back to him led to the calls from the police, the search of my home and my being charged with money laundering. How nice.

It turned out that Tim was not such a big shot in terms

of his business. He was a little man in the company, not a big man. He did not own or co-own the offshore companies he said he did, but was instead one of their many employees, and one who was very good at fiddling the system and adjusting the books so that he could systematically steal from them over a very long time. He even stole from his fellow employees' charity fund. Only he got clumsy. When he paid for some sex stuff on his credit card, the strange name of the central London shop sent alarm bells ringing in the company's accounts department. It didn't take long for the rest of Tim's misdemeanours to unravel, and for me to be caught up in them.

I had never really been in trouble – certainly not this level of trouble – and, after I had been to the station and given my statement, I thought that everything would be set straight and that I'd be in the clear. I didn't know then but the system takes for ever to run its course and can be easily manipulated from both sides, and months after I've given my statement and interviews, I receive the police case summary and later reports. It's many pages long so I'll have to give you a few of its highlights: it claims that I was '1.1 million pounds in debt', something they never even asked me about, that I 'treated the interview with distain', that I 'engaged in self admitted seedy activities', 'claimed to have been paid about double the figures the police are aware of at this time, and appears to be proud of the matter', 'the defence had been concocted to suit the circumstances', suggesting my solicitor's involvement. That I was basically engaged in 'clipping clients' (a term to mean street-level deception). But the most difficult of all to read was, 'What was seen at his sordid flat has been officially reported to Charing Cross Police station because it is strongly suspected that he may be involved with children and vulnerable adults.' This was so plainly untrue that it seemed clear that there may have been some attempt by the police to either discredit me or a witness in front of the jury. And then there was an eleventh-hour new report suggesting I was potentially violent. All the claims were investigated and there were no facts to support any of these statements; in fact, no report was even made to the police or any child protection unit and the officer accidentally misread a credit report that gave him the impression I was 1.1 million in debt rather than in credit – I'll let you draw your own conclusions.

Finally I was charged under the 2002 Money Laundering Act, all because of my involvement with Tim and the money he had embezzled from his company. If found guilty I was facing having all my assets taken away from me, and a jail sentence of between two and four years.

I sank into a terrible depression. It was spring 2007. I was told that I would stand trial in February 2008. My accounts were frozen as there were suggestions that I ran brothels. I felt utterly paralysed. Jennifer didn't know what to do. It was one thing for her having a naughty boy for a lover, but quite another trying to plan a future with someone who might go to prison and who has been accused of unmentionable things. It was too much for me to take: Tim's deception meant that I may go to jail, and my life seemed to be crashing down around me. I couldn't contemplate my future, it all looked so bleak. Plus, I've gone. I've disappeared. I'm like the walking dead.

We would go out to restaurants and Jennifer would wave her hand in front of my face and say to me: 'Andrew. Where are you? Come back.' All I could think about was my case. I had to take my house off the market, because, as one of my assets, it was potentially liable for reclamation. I had to begin escorting once again, now that my accounts were frozen, something I was ill equipped to do with my confidence at rock bottom. Weirdly, it was at exactly this time that I won the UK Escort of the Year Award at the Erotic Awards for my work with the poor and disabled. Later, the irony was not lost on me or Jennifer, because during the twelve months I held the crown I was so depressed I think we had sex twice. That must be a record in the sex industry.

The Erotic Awards are like the Oscars for the sex industry. How do you measure who is the best escort in the UK in any given year? How is it judged? Well, of course in many ways it can't be – but it's an indication of something. I was touched and pleased to be made Escort of the Year and I still like to look at my trophy – a golden cock with wings!

Jennifer and I went to California with her family as we had planned. The tickets had already been bought. Jennifer thought that driving along route 101 under the huge Californian skies might help me break out of my depression. It didn't. I remember being in Big Sur, one of the most beautiful stretches of coastline in the world, and only half-seeing it. It was like I couldn't take it in. All I could think about was the case. Meanwhile, I was dragging Jennifer down too. I kept saying to her, let's finish. Let's call it a day. I knew she wanted to be free of me and my troubles, but I also knew that she didn't want to desert me in my time of need. For months we continued like this.

Finally, we agreed it was better that we part. I clearly could not be her boyfriend and she could not provide the support I needed to get me through the ordeal of the trial I faced. We decided we should stop pretending we were a couple. We could then at least stop feeling guilty about each other and get on with trying to repair ourselves. I wasn't as devastated by the break-up with Jennifer as I was with Hannah – there was just too much going on in my life, the court case was taking up all of my head space – and the thought of being alone to sort myself out was really quite appealing. There was a little bit of regret too – I couldn't help but feel that I could be letting go one of the best things that had happened to me – but I was too messed up to be able to be fully present in the relationship. I needed to try and sort myself out.

This healing process was helped for me by seeing my last ever client. It was Cheryl. I had stopped seeing Cheryl when I started travelling with Hannah, then I had seen her a few times once I had picked up my business again in 2006. But she had stopped calling me at just about the time that Jennifer and I first began dating. She was changing her life, she told me on the telephone, and moving away from Essex (which I took as a euphemism to mean she was retiring to the Costa del Sol). We spoke affectionately about our time together and wished each other well. I remember thinking: good old Cheryl, I wonder what the next chapter of her life will be like.

It was almost exactly a year on from our last conversation when Cheryl rang me out of the blue and asked if we could see each other one last time. 'I didn't move away, sweetheart,' she told me, 'but I'll explain everything when we see each other. If you will come and see me.'

I told her I would. 'You'll be my last job, Cheryl,' I said.

'Oh yes?' she replied, her voice tinkling with laugher. 'I've heard that before. You're a born escort, darling. Much too talented to give up. Or are you in love again?'

'Not in love,' I replied. 'But my life has changed too. I'll explain when I see you. We'll have plenty to talk about, won't we?'

'Talking!' said Cheryl. 'Me? That'll be a first.' She laughed and though she was being saucy, I could hear that something in her voice had changed.

Cheryl had cancer. 'It's serious, too,' she told me when I arrived at her house. 'Right in the heart. Or at least all through my blood. Same thing more or less. I'm going to stop taking the drugs. I'm off soon, darling.'

I realized this was a last treat for a dying woman. She spoke so bravely and plainly about her fate that I was almost moved to tears. I didn't cry, though, because that was not why Cheryl had called me. My job was to cheer her up. To touch and lick her body and to make her come one last time. Only as I began to undress her, she stopped me. 'It's not working,' she said. 'I'm not wet. Remember how wet I used to go? It's the drugs,' she added. 'Let's just talk a bit more.' And so I told her what had been going on in my life. Every so often I asked her if I was talking too much but she said no. She said it was good to hear about what someone else had been going through, though she was sorry for my troubles. Then an odd thing happened. I heard myself say: 'Shall we pray?' as I put my hand on Cheryl's shoulder.

Cheryl laughed softly. 'I'm a lapsed Catholic,' she said, tears in her eyes. 'If you can believe that. Irish grand-parents. But I don't know if I can pray. I'm not sure about anyone being up there. But if you believe he can help, then you talk to him. I'll listen.'

'I don't know,' I said. 'This morning I would have sworn he wasn't. That there was no one. Nothing. But I don't know. Somehow it just feels like it might help us.'

I began praying aloud, quietly, my left hand on Cheryl's

shoulder and my right stroking her hair. I felt an incredible calmness come over both of us. The police report about my supposedly squalid life, words that had been echoing around my head twenty-four hours a day since I first read them, somehow grew quiet and receded for the first time. I began to feel like I could be healed again. Cheryl too looked at peace. Somehow my words had meant something to her, or perhaps it was simply that I was touching her. Who knows? She was having her own thoughts and dealing with something much more profound. She was facing the end of her life and doing it with tremendous courage. I admired her.

I also felt grateful to her. You're not supposed to call up a prostitute and spend a couple of precious hours with him when you're dying of cancer. Prostitutes aren't supposed to pray with their clients. Somehow, although I haven't touched Cheryl sexually, this different kind of laying on of hands has had a tremendous effect on us both. We hugged each other when my prayer came to an end. We hugged each other tight, hardly speaking, and when it was time for me to go, for the first time in ten years of escorting, a miracle occurred: I refused the money Cheryl had paid me for the session and refused any kind of payment at all.

The court case was set to begin in February 2008. From October till February, although still fighting depression, I also had a new kind of energy, and it was one that was born entirely from my determination to win my case and prove my innocence.

I was so proud of the people who stood up in court to support me. Caterina, now happy and with a boyfriend, had to be carried up the steps to the court in her wheelchair to give evidence about the work she and I did together. It was tremendously brave of her to talk openly in public, but she did it and moved the entire court to tears. A barrister with an extremely high-profile job also took the stand as a witness in my defence. So did a working police officer, my builder, a judge, a journalist, an accountancy partner, leading academics and old and new friends. It was so important to me and to the case that everyone was willing to back me up, even though for some it was potentially difficult to back an escort so publicly. But they showed all their mettle.

I was lucky with my witnesses. They proved not only to be invaluable in my court case but in my life. I was lucky too with my barrister, a woman I can only describe as a cross between a catwalk model and a Doberman pinscher (my solicitor, meanwhile, reminds me of Obi-Wan Kenobi). But if I was lucky with my defence team and my witnesses at the trial, I was equally unlucky with the judge overseeing it, who I felt was extremely biased throughout the case and especially in his summing up of what had gone on. My barrister made objections about the judge's behaviour but it was only when the prosecutor – amazingly – stood in support of the defence and complained that the trial was unfair because of the bias that the judge was dismissed! Why did the prosecutor do such a thing, when the judge was trying to throw the case in his favour? I don't know. I like to think it was simply because he was a good man with integrity. I couldn't quite believe – the trial had collapsed, because the prosecutor saw bias in the judge against an escort. I felt elation, sure, but it was only temporary as I discovered that my case would be retried. However, it meant a lot to me that a judge was being held accountable for his prejudices. It makes me hope that things are changing, that sex workers may yet start to be taken seriously in the legal system.

I've discovered so much in ten years of escorting about us humans. It's been a wonderful roller coaster but I want to stop this ride and get off. A retrial has been set for July 2008. As I write this book, I await my fate. I may yet lose everything. I may yet go to jail. I may yet lose my right to be able to say I am innocent. But I don't think I will lose my faith in human nature, nor in the mystery and wonder of sex.

Change Is Here To Stay

In July 2008 I went again to stand trial. I arrived only to discover that my case had been cancelled because the prosecution opted to present no evidence and declared 'the prospect of achieving a conviction to be unlikely'. I was acquitted. Sixteen long months after I first received that fateful phone call from the police, I was finally free, my innocence intact; the lead officer retired. The relief was unbelievable, but it also felt strangely anti-climactic. I had been worrying for months, ruining my health, and it was difficult to suddenly feel that it was all over, that something just as bad wasn't lurking round the corner, preparing to pounce.

That same day, just as I was turning into my street and about to unlock my front door, for the first time in ages without wondering how long I'd be able to do that, my phone rang. It was Innocence.

The timing was spooky, but then timing so often is. 'Andrew,' she said, as if we'd seen each other just the week before. 'I'm in Trafalgar Square, round the corner from you. Can you come and lend a hand?'

I laughed. 'Help with what?' I said. 'Fill helium balloons. We're doing a protest about private equity.'

Private equity? Of all the things to protest about, it seems to me that capitalism is not the worst evil, but still I was curious. 'What group are you with?' I asked.

'It's called PEAN,' she said. 'It stands for Private Equity Action Network. We're really going to kick up a storm. Come on. Come and help.'

With Innocence there is always something to fight, even if it's with helium balloons. At least she is out there fighting. At least she is part of something. At least she's using her voice. I made my way to Trafalgar Square where I found Innocence and her Anarchist Socialist Marxist sexy friends filling gold balloons shaped like numbers with helium. They were planning to spell out across the square numerically how much tax is lost from the purchase of Boots the chemist by a private equity firm that is loading it with debt. Of course they have a point. A huge amount of money has been lost – money that could have been used to do good – because such buyouts are allowed. But this was not my battle. I helped make tea and filled a few balloons, but after a little while I realized that I felt out of place among Innocence's crowd of protestors and so after saying my goodbyes I started to make my way home.

As I walked away I was struck by the feeling that I had done the wrong thing. Perhaps I should have stayed and shouted, I thought. Perhaps I should be with Innocence and her crazy, vocal gang raising my voice about good causes. I continued walking home as my phone rang. Finally, I picked it up. It was Innocence.

'Forgot to say,' she said. 'I've got a fab duo job on tonight. Would love to do it with you.'

I told her that I'm retired. I told her this time it was for good.

Innocence didn't miss a beat when I said this. 'Oh no, darling,' she said, quick as a knife, her voice never surer. 'One never retires. One just takes a break. You'll be back,' she added. 'Mark my words, you'll be back.'

Acknowledgements

I'd like to thank Xavier Leret and the very sexy and smart Emma Jacobs and all those in the IUSW – the International Union of Sex Workers. You can contact them at branch.secretary@IUSW.org